I0518443

SERVICE DOGS
— FOR —
MENTAL HEALTH

SERVICE DOGS
—— FOR ——
MENTAL HEALTH

Breaking Barriers,
Building Independence,
Transforming Lives

FRANK COHEN

Service Dogs for Mental Health: Breaking Barriers, Building Independence, Transforming Lives

Published by Frank D Cohen

Copyright © 2025 by Frank D Cohen

All rights reserved. Neither this book nor any parts within it may be sold or reproduced in any form or by any electronic or mechanical means, including information storage and retrieval systems, without permission in writing from the author. The only exception is by a reviewer, who may quote short excerpts in a review.

Library of Congress Control Number: 2025945025

ISBN (paperback): 9798998501012
eISBN: 9798998501005

Foreword

By Gregg Laskoski

WHEN FRANK COHEN AND his dog, Gracie, walked into K9 Partners for Patriots for his first training class, he sat quietly with five other veterans. He had seen and heard enough to believe there might be a better path ahead with a service dog by his side. Each one walked in quietly. It was a new environment, the size of a warehouse or hangar. And while all had visited before starting and even watched several training classes, their first few weeks always bring collective stress and anxiety, not only for the veterans but the dogs that sense it too. Frank & Gracie were no exception.

K9P4P helps veterans struggling with Post Traumatic Stress Disorder (PTSD), Traumatic Brain Injury (TBI), or Military Sexual Trauma (MST). We help veterans find a positive path with a service dog by their side, helping them mitigate their disabilities. When veterans find us, it's generally after they've exhausted a variety of other options that failed. So their apprehension is understandable. *Will this really work for me?*

In the beginning, Frank was uneasy. At one point –he'll tell you—he was overwhelmed by the responsibility. Danny, a classmate, encouraged him to 'see it through to the finish.' Danny said he gave Frank some tips, but the most important thing was listening. "I was just there for him."

Another classmate, Woody, said the class became closer each week. He said he was scared at the beginning because "the trainers knew if you hadn't trained your dog when you returned each week. I talked to Frank every morning, and sometimes we'd meet on Sunday because there's a K9P4P grad who sells coffee at the flea market. Each week, our group grew closer together. We started looking at each other, realizing that we're all feeling better… It was like, 'Look at me, I'm getting out again!'

"So, we got through it. I felt like I finally had something that was helping me cope with what I went through." (Woody survived not one, but two plane crashes.) "I couldn't take people. Couldn't take the crowds." Not long ago, he said he'd wait in a restaurant for a certain table to become available; otherwise, he wouldn't be seated. Not anymore. "Now with Ruby, I can go anywhere. I'm the happiest person in the world."

One last point to share… Frank & Woody, accompanied by Gracie and Ruby, served as stellar ambassadors for K9 Partners for Patriots when the Hernando County (FL) Board of County Commissioners (BOCC) issued a resolution honoring National PTSD Awareness Day (June 27, 2025) and K9P4P's program for veterans. Woody jokingly introduced his Service dog, Ruby (a poodle) as a German Shepherd and wryly noted that when it comes to the plane crashes he survived, "the Navy just considers them hard landings."

Frank told the BOCC and viewing audience that he had struggled his entire adult life with PTSD, TBI. "It was only by the grace of God that I found K9 Partners for Patriots. I will tell you that like many of our veterans, I was out of time and out of hope."

Gracie changed all that. To borrow from Paul Simon's powerful song, 'Like a bridge over troubled water, she will ease his mind.'

If you want to learn more about the extraordinary mental health benefits of service dogs, you won't find a more candid or practical discussion than what Frank has put together. Some might cringe at this expression, but I'd venture to say he's a 'thought leader' and what makes him especially effective is his willingness to share his own doubts, concerns, and fears he encountered along the way. He's a problem solver, and this book is his way of helping others understand their options and find their path forward with a four-legged partner.

Gregg Laskoski is the Communications Director for K9 Partners for Patriots, Brooksville, FL.

Preface

THE MOMENT THAT CHANGED everything happened in a Publix parking lot. I was preparing to go grocery shopping—something most people do without a second thought—when the familiar grip of a panic attack began to close in. As I opened the back of my SUV to get Grace, my psychiatric service dog, she did something unexpected: she refused to budge. While I'll never know exactly what goes through that remarkable brain of hers, it felt like she sensed what I was experiencing and decided to keep me safe. We left without entering the store and returned another day, when I was better equipped to handle it.

That was when I truly understood that Grace wasn't just a well-trained dog. She was about to become the key to reclaiming a life that had been constrained by invisible wounds for decades.

My journey with complex PTSD, anxiety, and traumatic brain injury began during what was supposed to be a lifetime career in the United States Navy. Though my service was brief—cut short by a medical discharge—the trauma I endured during that time would echo through my entire adult life. As a hospital corpsman, I was exposed to life-threatening situations that no amount of training can truly prepare you for. I lost friends during hostile engagements, helped wounded Marines while waiting for medevac, and witnessed the kind of suffering that burrows deep into your psyche. The termination of my military career took more than just my physical capabilities; it severed me from the first real brotherhood and camaraderie I'd ever experienced. For someone who had planned to be a lifer, that loss compounded the original trauma in ways that would affect my relationships and work life for years to come.

Before Grace, simple activities that others took for granted felt insurmountable. Meeting new people triggered hypervigilance that left me exhausted. Public places became obstacle courses of potential threats rather than spaces for normal interaction. I avoided social gatherings, struggled with professional networking, and found myself increasingly isolated by my own survival mechanisms.

Like many veterans, I tried numerous paths toward healing. Traditional therapy helped somewhat. Medications provided partial relief. But nothing felt like a real solution—until I witnessed a transformation that made me reconsider everything I thought I knew about managing mental health conditions.

A fellow veteran and I used to share our struggles, finding comfort in knowing we weren't alone in our battles. Then he entered the K9 Partners for Patriots program. Over the six months following his graduation with his service dog, I watched this man transform. He seemed more confident, more relaxed, more present in his own life. He had found something I desperately wanted but wasn't sure I deserved.

That last point—deserving—nearly kept me from applying. The guilt was overwhelming. Surely there were other veterans who needed this more, who had served longer, who had "earned" it in ways I hadn't. It took several conversations with the compassionate staff at K9P4P to help me understand that trauma doesn't operate on a merit system. A short enlistment can produce profound wounds. Invisible disabilities are no less real than visible ones. Eventually, I pushed past the guilt and submitted my application.

The training journey itself became transformative in unexpected ways. I spent the first three months in basic obedience training, learning the fundamentals alongside Grace. Then came six months at K9P4P, where I learned not just how to have and care for a service dog, but how to train one. The program's philosophy of teaching veterans to train their own dogs meant I was gaining knowledge in canine behavior, learning theory, and task development. After graduation, I spent another six months with an additional trainer, learning more advanced tasking. By the time we were done, Grace had become an excellent service dog, and I had unexpectedly become a pretty competent service dog trainer myself.

But that journey wasn't without moments of doubt. About two months into the program, I became terribly overwhelmed and decided to quit. The weight of the responsibility, the public attention, the constant training—it all felt like too much. I had even found another veteran willing to take Gracie, convinced I wasn't cut out for this. That's when Danny, my battle buddy in the program, stepped in. Danny and his service dog, Zeus, were going through the same training, and we would graduate together. He talked me through that dark moment, helping me find the confidence to continue. He reminded me that this was my mission, and if nothing else, I am mission-oriented. This kind of support—the understanding that can only be shared by people with shared experiences—became as vital to my success as the training itself.

Today, I feel more confident meeting new people and going to public places. In some respects, having Grace creates an interesting dynamic—she refocuses people's attention from me to her, which paradoxically makes social interactions easier. The hypervigilance that once exhausted me has been replaced by trust in Grace's ability to monitor our environment. I can focus on conversations rather than escape routes.

I wrote this book because the transformation that followed needs to be understood—not just the inspiring parts, but the complete picture. Yes, Grace has given me independence and confidence I hadn't experienced in decades. But I wish I'd known about the challenges too: the expense of maintaining a working dog, the constant ongoing training, the end of spontaneous errands, and the relentless public attention that comes with having a dog in traditionally dog-free spaces. These realities don't diminish the value of the partnership, but understanding them beforehand helps create realistic expectations.

Perhaps most importantly, I wrote this book to address two critical issues that affect our entire community. First, the persistent disbelief we face because our disabilities aren't visible. Unlike someone in a wheelchair or being led by a guide dog for blindness, those of us with psychiatric service dogs often hear the skepticism in people's voices when they question whether we "really" need our dogs.

I'll never forget walking into a restaurant while out of town—already a challenging situation for someone with my conditions—when the hostess yelled at me to get my dog out, saying no dogs were allowed. I tried to explain that Grace wasn't a pet but a trained service dog, but she wouldn't listen. I ended up leaving, humiliated by the public confrontation. These experiences aren't rare; they're part of the reality of having an invisible disability in a world that expects disabilities to be obvious.

Second, the growing problem of fake service dogs—people who lie about disabilities and misrepresent pets as service animals. When these untrained dogs misbehave in public, they create lasting negative impressions. As the saying goes, we tend to judge any group by its least favorable members.

My work with K9 Partners for Patriots as a board member stems from a principle I learned in 12-step fellowships: "You only keep what you have by giving it away." My father taught me that if you know something that can help someone else, you have an obligation to share it. Having received this life-changing gift, I feel a strong commitment to give back to other veterans what was so freely given to me. This book is part of that commitment—a way to share hard-won knowledge with those who need it.

I hope this comprehensive guide will serve multiple purposes: helping prospective handlers make informed decisions, assisting mental health professionals in supporting their clients, educating businesses and community members about genuine service dog partnerships, and ultimately creating a more inclusive society where invisible disabilities are recognized and respected.

This book wouldn't exist without the support of many people. My deepest gratitude goes to my wife, Susan, who lived with my disabilities for over 30 years before Grace arrived, and who continues to adapt to our new reality with patience and love. To my friend Mick and his dog Bruno, who first showed me what was possible. To Danny and Zeus—my battle buddy and his partner—who kept me going when I wanted to quit; your brotherhood meant everything. To the entire staff at K9 Partners for Patriots, who believed I deserved help even when I didn't. And to Julie at Patriot Service Dogs, Inc., whose expertise and friendship have been invaluable.

Finally, to Grace herself—my partner, my lifeline, and my teacher in ways I never expected. She may never read these words, but every page reflects something she's taught me about resilience, trust, and the profound bond between human and dog when both are committed to the work of healing.

If you're reading this book—whether you're considering a service dog, a professional seeking to understand, or a community member wanting to be more inclusive—know that behind every statistic and legal citation is a story like mine: someone trying to reclaim their life from invisible wounds. My hope is that this knowledge helps you in whatever way you need it.

Frank Cohen
Spring Hill, Florida
2025

About the Author

FRANK COHEN BRINGS A rare blend of personal experience, professional expertise, and research acumen to psychiatric service dog advocacy. A Navy Hospital Corpsman veteran and healthcare data scientist, Mr. Cohen has spent over 40 years applying advanced analytics, artificial intelligence, and statistical modeling to healthcare challenges. His background allows him to critically evaluate and synthesize scientific research with precision, skills he now applies to the growing body of evidence on service dog effectiveness.

As a consultant and expert in computational statistics, Mr. Cohen approaches service dog research with the same rigor he brings to large-scale healthcare studies. He emphasizes evidence-based practices, drawing on peer-reviewed literature to inform training models, program design, and policy development. His analytical perspective helps distinguish anecdotal claims from measurable outcomes, an essential distinction in a field where scientific validation is still evolving.

Mr. Cohen's personal connection to the topic deepens his impact. Since 2023, he has been partnered with Grace, his psychiatric service dog. Living with PTSD, anxiety, and traumatic brain injury, he understands firsthand the benefits and challenges of daily life with a service dog. This real-world perspective, combined with his role on the Board of Directors at K9 Partners for Patriots, allows him to speak credibly about both individual needs and systemic solutions.

His military medical experience further informs his understanding of disability accommodation and behavioral health interventions, particularly for veterans. He actively works to bridge the gap between academic research and practical implementation, ensuring service dog programs are grounded in solid data, not just good intentions.

Mr. Cohen's commitment to evidence-based advocacy supports improved training standards, fraud prevention, and funding accessibility. His work helps mental health professionals, policymakers, and community organizations make informed decisions that benefit both handlers and the public. As a researcher, veteran, and service dog handler, he offers a unique and credible voice in advancing the role of psychiatric service dogs in mental health care.

Table of Contents

Service Dogs for Mental Health: A Comprehensive Guide

Breaking Barriers, Building Independence, Transforming Lives

A detailed resource for mental health professionals, educators, individuals with lived experience, families, and community members

Introduction: A Personal Journey

My name is Frank Cohen, and I want to share something that has fundamentally changed my life. After decades of living with complex post-traumatic stress disorder (PTSD) and symptoms from a traumatic brain injury (TBI) sustained during my Navy service, I believed I had tried every available treatment option. Traditional and cognitive behavioral therapy helped to some degree. Medications provided partial relief. But it wasn't until July 2023, when I was partnered with my psychiatric service dog, that I truly understood what independence and confidence could feel like again.

I'm not sharing this to diminish the importance of traditional mental health treatment—I continue to work with mental health professionals and consider my service dog a complement to, not a replacement for, comprehensive care. Rather, I want to highlight an option that remains misunderstood, underutilized, and often inaccessible to those who could benefit from it most.

The Scope of Need

The numbers tell a story of profound unmet need. According to the National Institute of Mental Health, nearly one in five U.S. adults lives with a mental illness[32] – that's over 57 million people. Among veterans, the statistics are even more stark: the Department of Veterans Affairs reports that between 11-20% of veterans who served in Operations Iraqi Freedom and Enduring Freedom experience PTSD in a given year [33]. Add to this the millions living with severe anxiety disorders, major depression, autism spectrum disorders, and other mental health conditions that significantly limit daily functioning, and we're looking at a population in the tens of millions who might benefit from psychiatric service dog partnerships.

Yet despite this enormous need, only a tiny fraction of these individuals have access to properly trained psychiatric service dogs. There's no central registry tracking exact numbers, but estimates suggest fewer than 20,000 psychiatric service dog teams are currently working in the United States. This gap between need and access represents millions of people who might regain independence, reduce reliance on emergency services, and participate more fully in their communities – if only they had access to accurate information and appropriate resources.

The Critical Knowledge Gap

This guide exists to address a dangerous knowledge gap that affects everyone involved in the psychiatric service dog community. Mental health professionals often don't know how to advise clients who ask about service dogs, sometimes dismissing the option entirely or providing outdated information. Prospective handlers must navigate a confusing landscape of legitimate programs mixed with scams, often spending thousands of dollars on dogs that will never be able to perform true service work.

Business owners and educators, wanting to comply with the law but unsure of their responsibilities, may either deny legitimate access rights or inadvertently allow fake service dogs that erode public trust. Community members, seeing more dogs in public spaces, often don't understand the difference between service dogs, emotional support animals, and pets, leading to inappropriate interactions that can disrupt life-saving work.

Perhaps most troubling, the rise of fake service dogs—untrained pets wearing purchased vests—has created a crisis of legitimacy that makes life harder for every genuine handler. When businesses have negative experiences with misbehaving fake service dogs, they become skeptical of all service dog teams. This skepticism leads to access challenges, confrontations, and discrimination that can make public participation impossible for people who rely on their service dogs to function each day.

> **REALITY CHECK:** Service dogs typically work 8-10 years. Plan for retirement, succession, and end-of-life decisions.

What's at Stake?

The consequences of this knowledge gap are real and devastating. I've known veterans who spent their limited resources on dogs from fraudulent "registries," only to discover their untrained pets couldn't provide the support they urgently needed. I've seen handlers denied access to medical care, education, and employment because gatekeepers didn't understand their legal responsibilities. I've watched partnerships fail—not because of poor training or mismatched teams, but because handlers weren't prepared for the lifestyle changes and ongoing commitment that service dog partnerships require.

Without accurate information, people with mental health disabilities face unnecessary barriers to independence. They may spend years on waiting lists for programs that aren't right for their needs, invest in training approaches that are unlikely to succeed, or give up entirely on an option that could transform their lives. Meanwhile, their families struggle to offer support without understanding how service dogs might help, employers miss chances to accommodate valuable workers, and communities fall short of creating inclusive environments where all members can thrive.

Why This Book, Why Now?

When I began preparing to pursue a psychiatric service dog, I dove into research with the thoroughness that my background in data science had trained me to apply to complex problems. I read more than 50 books cover to cover, consumed countless blog posts and podcasts, watched training videos, and studied academic research papers on service dogs for mental health conditions. What I discovered was both enlightening and frustrating.

The existing literature was remarkably monolithic. There were excellent training manuals focused solely on technique and methodology. Detailed academic studies explored canine cognition, behavioral science, or genetics. Legal guides addressed rights and regulations. Personal memoirs shared individual experiences. Each resource offered valuable insights within its narrow scope, but none provided the comprehensive guidance that prospective handlers actually need.

What was missing was a resource that addressed the full spectrum of issues psychiatric service dog owners must navigate—from understanding the science behind the training to managing the financial realities, from knowing your legal rights to handling the social challenges of increased visibility, from selecting legitimate programs to planning for your dog's eventual retirement. I wrote this book to fill that critical gap.

As a graduate and board member of K9 Partners for Patriots, an organization dedicated to training service dogs for veterans with service-related conditions, I've witnessed the transformation that occurs when the right person meets the right dog with proper training. I've also seen the barriers, misconceptions, and gaps in knowledge that prevent many from accessing this life-changing resource—gaps that could be addressed with more comprehensive information.

What makes this guide unique is the intersection of perspectives it brings. As someone living with PTSD and TBI who partners daily with a psychiatric service dog, I understand the lived reality of these partnerships—the profound benefits and the unexpected challenges. As a board member of a service dog organization, I've gained insight into the training process, organizational hurdles, and systemic barriers that limit access. As a data scientist with over 40 years of experience in statistical analysis and research, I bring a critical eye to evaluating claims about service dog effectiveness, separating anecdote from evidence.

This combination allows me to address questions that single-perspective resources often overlook: What does the research actually say about psychiatric service dog effectiveness? How can you distinguish legitimate training programs from scams? What are the daily realities—both positive and challenging—of living with a service dog? How can communities foster environments where service dog teams can thrive? Most importantly, how do all these pieces fit together to help you make informed decisions about this life-changing commitment?

A Path Forward

This guide is my attempt to bridge those gaps with comprehensive, practical information grounded in both evidence and experience. Whether you're a mental health professional seeking to better serve your clients, an individual wondering if a psychiatric service dog might help your situation, a family member trying to understand this option, or a community member working to create more inclusive spaces, this resource aims to provide the detailed information you need to make informed decisions and take effective action.

The statistics are sobering: while mental health conditions affect millions of Americans, only a fraction have access to psychiatric service dogs. The training is intensive, the costs are significant, and the legal landscape can be confusing. Yet for those who navigate this path successfully, the results can be profound—not just in symptom management, but in reclaiming independence, rebuilding confidence, and reconnecting with community.

Throughout this book, I'll share not only inspiring success stories but also the hard truths about service dog partnerships. You'll learn about the legal framework that protects handlers' rights and the practical realities of exercising those rights in sometimes unwelcoming environments. You'll understand the science behind how these partnerships work and the training methods that create reliable working dogs. You'll explore the financial, emotional, and lifestyle commitments involved, and how to assess your readiness for them.

Most importantly, you'll gain the knowledge needed to be part of the solution—whether that means pursuing a service dog partnership yourself, supporting someone else on their journey, or simply becoming a more informed and inclusive member of your community. Ultimately, building a society where people with mental health disabilities can thrive requires all of us to understand, support, and advocate for the accommodations that make independence possible.

Let me share what I've learned, both as someone whose life has been transformed by this partnership and as someone working to make these opportunities available to others who need them. The journey isn't always easy, but for those who need it, it can be the difference between surviving and truly living.

How This Book Is Organized

This comprehensive guide is structured to serve multiple audiences while telling a complete story about psychiatric service dogs. Whether you're reading cover to cover or looking for specific information, understanding the organization will help you find the content most relevant to your needs.

Chapters 1-3 establish the essential foundation. Chapter 1 defines what makes a legitimate service dog and explores the eight categories of service animals, clarifying the key differences between service dogs and emotional support animals. Chapter 2 focuses on how psychiatric service dogs transform lives through trained tasks like interrupting panic attacks, retrieving medication, and responding to nightmares, supported by research on the science behind these partnerships. Chapter 3 offers a detailed analysis of legal rights and protections under the ADA, Fair Housing Act, and other relevant laws—crucial information for handlers, businesses, and institutions navigating access rights and accommodation responsibilities. These chapters are essential for anyone seeking to understand the nature, capabilities, and legal framework of psychiatric service dogs.

Chapters 4-5 form the practical framework of training realities. Chapter 4 presents the statistical realities of training and selection, with honest insights into success rates, costs, and the distinctions between professional programs and owner-training approaches. Chapter 5 delves into the sophisticated science behind service dog training, exploring the learning theory, conditioning principles, and systematic approaches that transform well-intentioned pets into reliable working medical equipment. Together, these chapters help readers understand both what training involves and why it's so demanding.

Chapters 6-7 shift to the lived experience of service dog partnership. Chapter 6 provides an unfiltered look at the day-to-day realities—from financial commitments and ongoing responsibilities to emergency planning and lifestyle changes. Chapter 7 addresses the complex social dimensions of partnership, including the challenge of increased public visibility, managing unwanted attention, and navigating the paradox of making invisible disabilities visible through service dog presence. These chapters are especially valuable for prospective handlers and those supporting someone considering a service dog, as they outline both the practical demands and social adjustments involved.

Chapters 8-9 explore extended partnership considerations and community support. Chapter 8 addresses advanced partnership planning including family dynamics, long-term commitment requirements, retirement preparation, and multi-dog household challenges—essential information for understanding the full lifecycle of service dog partnerships. Chapter 9 offers guidance for mental health professionals on integrating service dogs into treatment planning, practical advice for business owners and educators on fostering inclusive environments, and essential information for healthcare facilities on balancing accommodations with medical protocols.

Chapters 10-11 address current challenges and provide practical resources. Chapter 10 tackles the growing problem of fake service dogs and explores potential solutions, including enhanced education, state-level initiatives, and the debate around national certification possibilities. Chapter 11 offers extensive resources for further learning and support, from training organizations to legal advocacy groups, providing concrete next steps for individuals, professionals, and communities.

Chapter 12 brings together the book's themes with personal reflections on the transformative power of these partnerships, illustrated through stories that show the profound impact service dogs can have—not just on handlers, but on everyone they encounter.

The book concludes with a **Frequently Asked Questions** section that addresses common concerns, followed by a comprehensive **References** section for those interested in verifying claims or exploring further research.

Throughout, you'll find real-world examples, evidence-based research, practical insights drawn from personal experience, professional involvement with service dog organizations, and extensive exploration of best practices. While each chapter builds on the previous content, most can also stand alone as resources for specific questions or situations you may face.

CHAPTER 1

Understanding Service Dogs: Definitions and Legal Framework

What Constitutes a Service Dog?

The confusion often begins with terminology. In everyday conversation, people frequently use "service dog," "therapy dog," and "emotional support animal" interchangeably. But these distinctions matter greatly in both legal and practical terms; they determine access rights, housing protections, and what questions people can legally ask..

Under the Americans with Disabilities Act, a service animal is explicitly defined as a dog individually trained to work or perform tasks for a person with a disability. [4] This definition contains several critical elements that distinguish genuine service dogs from other categories of working animals.

Individual Training for Specific Tasks

The keyword here is *tasks*—plural, specific, and directly related to the person's disability. A psychiatric service dog isn't simply a well-behaved pet that provides comfort through companionship. These animals undergo extensive training to perform specific behaviors that directly mitigate their handler's disability-related challenges.

For someone with PTSD, this might include searching a room before the handler enters, creating physical barriers in crowded spaces, or interrupting nightmares through specific wake-up protocols. For individuals with severe anxiety disorders, trained tasks could involve guiding them to exits during panic attacks, retrieving medication during episodes, or providing deep pressure therapy through trained positioning.

My service dog performs several specific tasks tailored to my conditions. When she senses my anxiety escalating—through changes in my breathing, posture, or other subtle cues she's learned to recognize—she nudges me in a specific way to prompt me to use coping strategies before reaching a crisis point. In crowded environments that trigger my PTSD, she's trained to position herself between me and other people, creating a buffer that helps me move through public spaces more comfortably.

> "Service dogs undergo extensive training to perform specific behaviors that directly mitigate their handler's disability-related challenges."

These behaviors don't emerge naturally from a well-socialized pet. Each response required months of targeted training, consistent reinforcement, and ongoing maintenance to ensure reliability in high-stress situations.

The Disability Connection

The ADA requires that a person have a qualifying disability and that the dog's trained tasks directly relate to that disability. This creates an essential distinction from emotional support animals, which provide comfort through companionship but are not required to perform specific tasks.

For psychiatric service dogs, qualifying disabilities typically include PTSD, severe anxiety disorders, major depressive disorder, bipolar disorder, autism spectrum disorders, and other mental health conditions that substantially limit major life activities. The key is demonstrating that specific trained tasks address functional limitations caused by the disability.

Service Dogs vs. Emotional Support Animals: Critical Distinctions

This distinction affects every aspect of how these animals are treated under the law, and understanding it can prevent significant legal and practical problems.

Psychiatric Service Dogs

Psychiatric service dogs, by contrast, are trained to perform specific tasks that directly address their handler's disability-related challenges. Because of this training and their essential role in their handler's daily functioning, they receive complete protection under the ADA.

This means psychiatric service dogs can accompany their handlers into restaurants, stores, workplaces, public transportation, and virtually all public accommodations.[2] They're protected in housing regardless of pet policies or breed restrictions.[5] Airlines must accommodate service dogs in the cabin without additional fees.[12]

The distinction matters practically as well as legally. When asked, "Is that a service dog?" in a restaurant or store, I can answer definitively "Yes" and follow up with information about her trained tasks. Someone with an emotional support animal cannot make these same claims or expect the same accommodation.

Emotional Support Animals

Emotional support animals provide comfort through companionship. They don't require specific training beyond basic pet behavior, and their therapeutic value comes from the general benefits of animal companionship—reduced isolation, increased motivation for self-care, and the psychological comfort of a loving relationship.

ESAs have minimal legal protections. They're generally allowed in housing that otherwise prohibits pets (under the Fair Housing Act),[5] but they have no public access rights. Airlines are no longer required to accommodate emotional support animals[12], and businesses can exclude them from their premises.

Therapy Dogs

Therapy dogs represent another category often confused with service dogs but serve a completely different purpose. These animals are trained to provide comfort, affection, and emotional support to multiple people in settings such as hospitals, nursing homes, schools, disaster areas, and courtrooms. Unlike service dogs that work for one specific handler, therapy dogs work with their volunteer handlers to support others—patients recovering from surgery, children learning to read, or trauma survivors processing difficult experiences.

Therapy dogs receive professional training focused on temperament, social skills, and appropriate behavior around strangers in a variety of environments. They must be calm, friendly, confident, and enjoy interacting with many different people. However, therapy dogs are not trained to perform specific tasks for individuals with disabilities, nor do they have public access rights under the ADA. They are permitted only in facilities that have explicitly invited them and cannot accompany their handlers into restaurants, stores, or other public accommodations. When a therapy dog isn't actively working in an approved facility, it has the same legal status as any pet.

This distinction is crucial: therapy dogs help others feel better, while psychiatric service dogs perform specific, trained tasks to help their individual handlers manage disability-related challenges.

Understanding the Eight Categories of Service Dogs

While this guide focuses on psychiatric service dogs, understanding the broader landscape helps contextualize their role within service animal work more generally. The range of service dog specialties reflects the wide variety of functional limitations that disabilities can create, and recognizing these categories illustrates both the sophistication of service dog training and the specific nature of the work these animals perform.

Guide Dogs assist individuals who are blind or have severe visual impairments by navigating obstacles and providing mobility support. They represent the oldest and most widely recognized category of service animals, with training programs dating back to World War I. Guide dogs learn complex navigation skills, including obstacle avoidance, traffic assessment, and intelligent disobedience—the ability to refuse commands that would place their handler in danger. They must master tasks such as finding doors, stairs, elevators, and specific locations while maintaining awareness of overhead obstacles, ground hazards, and moving traffic.

Hearing Dogs alert individuals who are deaf or hard of hearing to important sounds like doorbells, alarms, or approaching vehicles. These dogs learn to distinguish between different sounds and respond with specific alerting behaviors that communicate the nature and urgency of each sound. They might nudge their handler and lead them to a ringing doorbell, provide a different alert for a smoke alarm, or use distinct signals to indicate approaching vehicles or other safety concerns.

Mobility Assistance Dogs help individuals with physical disabilities by providing stability, retrieving dropped items, operating light switches, or even pulling wheelchairs. These dogs must be physically strong enough to provide meaningful assistance while remaining gentle and precise in their movements. They learn complex tasks such as bracing to help handlers stand or maintain balance, retrieving specific items on command, opening and closing doors, activating emergency alert systems, and assisting with transfers from wheelchairs to beds or chairs.

Medical Alert Dogs are trained to detect specific medical conditions— such as seizures, diabetic episodes, or other health emergencies—and either alert their handler or summon help. These dogs often show a natural ability to detect physiological changes that precede medical events, though the mechanisms they use—whether scent detection, behavioral observation, or other sensory input—are not fully understood. Diabetic alert dogs, for example, can detect changes in blood sugar levels before their handlers experience symptoms, providing time for intervention that can prevent dangerous episodes.

Psychiatric Service Dogs perform tasks specifically related to mental health disabilities, which we'll explore in detail throughout this guide. These dogs represent one of the newest and fastest-growing categories of service animals, reflecting a growing understanding of mental health conditions and the functional limitations they can create. Unlike other service dog categories that primarily address physical challenges, psychiatric service dogs must respond to internal experiences and emotional states that may not have obvious external signs.

Autism Assistance Dogs help individuals on the autism spectrum with specific challenges such as sensory overload, social navigation, or safety concerns. These dogs often work with children, providing deep pressure therapy during sensory overload episodes, interrupting potentially harmful repetitive behaviors, and assisting with safety for individuals who may wander or fail to recognize environmental dangers. They can be trained to create physical barriers in crowded environments, offer grounding during sensory overload, and even track individuals who have wandered away from safe areas.

Allergy Detection Dogs are trained to identify and alert to specific allergens that could trigger dangerous reactions. These highly specialized dogs learn to detect trace amounts of substances—such as peanuts, shellfish, or other allergens—in environments where their handlers may encounter them. They provide life-saving early warnings that allow handlers to avoid exposure or prepare for potential allergic reactions.

Seizure Response Dogs are trained to assist during or after seizure episodes by providing stability, retrieving medication, or activating emergency alert systems. These dogs learn to recognize the onset of seizure activity and respond with specific behaviors designed to keep their handlers safe. They might position themselves to cushion falls, clear airways, retrieve emergency medications, activate alert systems, or provide stability and orientation assistance as handlers recover. Some seizure response dogs also develop the ability to predict seizures before they occur; however, this predictive ability cannot be reliably trained and appears to be a natural talent in certain dogs.

Each category requires specialized training protocols that can take months or even years to complete, and most service dogs are trained to work within only one specialty area. This specialization ensures that the training is thorough and that the dog's responses are reliable in the specific situations their handler will encounter.

The diversity of service dog work also illustrates why broad generalizations can be misleading. A guide dog's work is immediately visible to observers, while a psychiatric service dog's tasks may be entirely internal and invisible. A mobility assistance dog may be large and physically strong, while a medical alert dog might be quite small. Understanding these differences helps explain why the ADA focuses on a dog's training and tasks rather than appearance, breed, or visible indicators of the handler's disability.

These eight categories also demonstrate how service dog work has evolved as our understanding of disabilities and accommodation needs has grown. Guide dogs and hearing dogs represent the earliest forms of service animal work, while categories like psychiatric service dogs and allergy detection dogs reflect more recent recognition of how trained animals can address previously overlooked functional limitations. This evolution continues as research deepens our understanding of both animal capabilities and human accommodation needs.

Conditions That May Benefit from Psychiatric Service Dogs

While psychiatric service dogs can potentially benefit individuals with various mental health conditions—including PTSD, severe anxiety disorders, major depressive disorder, autism spectrum disorders, bipolar disorder, and dissociative disorders—the specific ways these partnerships address each condition's unique challenges deserve detailed exploration. Understanding which conditions may benefit requires careful consideration of how specific symptoms align with trainable tasks.

Post-Traumatic Stress Disorder (PTSD)

PTSD symptoms—hypervigilance, flashbacks, avoidance behaviors, and sleep disturbances—can be directly addressed through specific service dog tasks. The combination of environmental assessment, nightmare interruption, and grounding techniques makes psychiatric service dogs particularly well-suited for PTSD management.

It's important to note that our understanding of PTSD continues to evolve. The organization *By My Side* states, "PTSD is not a mental disorder, it's a physical injury to the brain!" This perspective reflects a growing recognition that trauma can cause measurable physiological changes in brain structure and function. This understanding can be crucial for veterans and others who may feel stigmatized by mental health labels, helping them see that their symptoms stem from physical changes rather than personal weakness or character flaws. That said, it's important to acknowledge that the DSM-5 and ICD-11 still classify PTSD as a mental health disorder, though both recognize its neurobiological basis.

Hypervigilance, a hallmark of PTSD, involves constant scanning for potential threats, which often leads to exhaustion and difficulty functioning in public spaces. Service dogs trained in environmental assessment can conduct systematic room searches and provide reassurance about the safety of an area, allowing handlers to shift mental energy from threat scanning to more productive activities.

Flashbacks and dissociative episodes, common in PTSD, can be interrupted through grounding techniques provided by trained service dogs. Their physical presence and specific interventions help handlers stay connected to the present during moments when past trauma intrudes on current experience.

Avoidant behaviors, often developed as coping mechanisms, can also be addressed through the confidence and support that service dogs offer. Handlers frequently report being able to engage in activities and visit places they had previously avoided when accompanied by their trained service dog.

Sleep disturbances, including nightmares and insomnia, often respond well to nightmare interruption and sleep assistance tasks performed by psychiatric service dogs. Improved sleep quality from these interventions can contribute significantly to overall symptom reduction and recovery.

Severe Anxiety Disorders

Panic disorder, generalized anxiety disorder, and social anxiety disorder can all benefit from service dog intervention, especially when anxiety symptoms significantly limit a person's ability to participate in work, school, or community activities.

Panic disorder, characterized by the sudden onset of intense anxiety symptoms, responds particularly well to the early detection and interruption techniques service dogs can provide. The ability to recognize escalating anxiety before it reaches panic levels allows for intervention that may prevent or lessen the severity of panic attacks.

Generalized anxiety disorder, marked by persistent worry and anxiety across multiple areas of life, can be addressed through grounding and reality orientation tasks. These tasks help handlers stay connected to the present moment instead of becoming overwhelmed by anxious thoughts about future possibilities.

Social anxiety disorder can benefit from social buffering and crowd navigation tasks that help handlers manage overwhelming social environments. The presence of a service dog often provides confidence and support, enabling greater social participation while also offering practical help with space management and social navigation.

Agoraphobia, often linked to panic disorder, can be addressed through environmental assessment and crowd navigation tasks that help handlers feel safer in public spaces. Systematic desensitization—gradually increasing public activities with the support of a service dog—can also contribute to reduced agoraphobic avoidance.

Major Depressive Disorder

For individuals with severe depression, service dogs can provide medication reminders, motivation for basic self-care tasks, and interruption of harmful behaviors. The daily care requirements of the dog can also offer structure and purpose during depressive episodes when motivation and energy are severely compromised.

The medication management assistance that service dogs provide is particularly valuable during severe depressive episodes, when cognitive function may be impaired and basic self-care tasks feel overwhelming. Regular medication compliance often contributes to better symptom management and recovery progress.

Motivation and activity encouragement from service dogs, driven by their daily care needs, can help counter the inactivity and isolation that often characterize severe depression. The responsibility of caring for another living being often offers purpose and structure that help handlers maintain basic functioning during difficult periods.

Sleep regulation assistance that service dogs offer through routine and sleep-related tasks can help address the sleep disturbances commonly associated with depression. Improved sleep patterns often support better mood regulation and overall symptom management.

The reduction in social isolation that often results from engaging in public activities with a service dog can help counter the withdrawal and loneliness associated with severe depression. The social facilitation that service dogs provide can help handlers maintain social connections that support recovery.

Autism Spectrum Disorders

Individuals on the autism spectrum may benefit from service dogs trained in sensory interruption, social navigation assistance, and safety-related tasks. The predictable routine and consistent companionship can also provide stability in an often unpredictable world.

Sensory overload management through specific interruption and grounding techniques can help individuals with autism navigate environments that might otherwise be overwhelming. Service dogs can be trained to recognize signs of sensory overload and provide targeted interventions that help regulate sensory input.

Social navigation assistance through crowd management and social buffering tasks can help individuals with autism participate in community activities that might otherwise be too overwhelming or confusing. The structure and predictability that service dogs provide can make social situations more manageable.

Routine and structure support from service dogs, established through their daily care needs and training schedules, can help individuals with autism maintain the consistency and predictability that often support optimal functioning.

Safety assistance through specialized tasks can help individuals with autism who may have difficulty recognizing or responding to environmental dangers. Service dogs can be trained to deliver specific safety interventions that address individual risk factors and safety concerns.

Bipolar Disorder

Service dogs can be trained to recognize signs of mood episodes and provide grounding, medication reminders, or other interventions that help maintain stability. The routine and structure that service dog care provides can also contribute to mood stability and episode prevention.

Mood episode recognition through specific behavioral indicators can offer early warning of developing manic or depressive episodes, allowing for earlier intervention and improved episode management. Service dogs can be trained to detect subtle changes in behavior, sleep patterns, or activity levels that may signal an approaching mood episode.

Medication compliance assistance is particularly important in managing bipolar disorder, where non-compliance often precipitates mood episodes. Service dogs trained in medication reminder and retrieval tasks can support the consistent medication use that promotes mood stability.

Routine maintenance, supported by the daily care requirements and training schedules of service dogs, can help provide the structure and consistency that support mood stability in bipolar disorder. Regular activity and responsibility can counter both the inactivity of depression and the chaotic energy of mania.

Sleep regulation assistance from service dogs becomes especially critical in bipolar disorder, where sleep disruption frequently triggers mood episodes. The routine and sleep-related tasks service dogs perform can help maintain sleep hygiene and support overall mood stability.

Dissociative Disorders

The grounding and reality orientation tasks that service dogs can provide are particularly relevant for individuals with dissociative identity disorder or other dissociative conditions, where connection to present reality and body awareness may be compromised.

Reality grounding through specific physical contact and sensory input can help individuals with dissociative disorders maintain present-moment awareness during episodes of dissociation. Service dogs can be trained to provide targeted sensory input that supports or restores reality orientation.

Body awareness assistance through deliberate physical contact and pressure can help individuals with dissociative disorders stay connected to their physical experience during episodes when body awareness is altered or absent.

Episode interruption through specific intervention techniques can help reduce the duration and intensity of dissociative episodes, allowing for quicker return to baseline functioning and less disruption from dissociative symptoms.

Safety assistance during dissociative episodes, when awareness and judgment may be impaired, can help prevent accidents or unsafe situations. Service dogs can be trained to provide tailored safety interventions that address the specific risks associated with dissociation.

The expanding understanding of how psychiatric service dogs can address the functional limitations caused by various mental health conditions continues to grow as training techniques advance and research documentation increases. The key factor in determining whether a psychiatric service dog might be beneficial is not the specific diagnosis, but the presence of functional limitations that can be addressed through specific, trainable tasks a dog can reliably perform.

The sophisticated tasks that psychiatric service dogs perform—from panic attack interruption to nightmare intervention—demonstrate that these partnerships are genuine medical accommodations rather than lifestyle preferences. The growing body of research documenting physiological changes, functional improvements, and social integration benefits offers compelling evidence for the therapeutic value of well-trained psychiatric service dogs across multiple domains of functioning. However, these benefits exist within a complex legal framework that protects handlers' rights and sets clear boundaries for accommodation. Understanding how these legal protections work in practice is essential for handlers who rely on them for daily independence and community participation.

CHAPTER 2

From Disability to Independence: Psychiatric Service Dog Interventions

Understanding Psychiatric Service Dog Tasks

The transformation created by psychiatric service dogs becomes clear when you understand their specific, trained tasks. These aren't abstract concepts; they're concrete behaviors that address real, daily challenges faced by people with mental health conditions. Yet for many, including mental health professionals, the world of psychiatric service dogs remains mysterious, misunderstood, or seen as a "nice to have" rather than "medically necessary."

The reality is quite different. Psychiatric service dogs perform highly specific, measurable tasks that directly address the functional limitations caused by mental health disabilities. These tasks are as concrete and essential as a guide dog navigating obstacles for someone who is blind or a seizure-alert dog detecting oncoming episodes for someone with epilepsy. The difference is that psychiatric service dog tasks often address invisible disabilities through interventions that may not be immediately apparent to others.

When I first learned about psychiatric service dogs, I struggled to understand how a dog could address the complex, internal experiences of PTSD, anxiety, and traumatic brain injury that had dominated my life for decades. The concept seemed too simple, too good to be true. How could an animal grasp the intricate web of hypervigilance, dissociation, and panic that characterized my daily existence? The answer, I discovered, lies not in the dog's intellectual understanding of these experiences but in their remarkable capacity to detect, respond to, and interrupt the physical manifestations of these conditions before they escalate beyond control.

Panic Attack Interruption and Management

For individuals with panic disorder or severe anxiety, trained dogs can recognize the early physiological signs of an approaching panic attack—changes in breathing pattern, heart rate, or body positioning that occur before the person is even consciously aware of the escalating situation. This early detection capability is one of the most valuable aspects of psychiatric service dog work, transforming reactive crisis management into proactive intervention.

The physiology of panic attacks follows predictable patterns that dogs can be trained to recognize with remarkable accuracy. As anxiety escalates, subtle changes in breathing rhythm, muscle tension, body temperature, and even scent often precede conscious awareness of rising panic. While humans may miss these early warning signs because they are focused on external stressors or internal thoughts, dogs can be trained to monitor these physiological indicators continuously.

My service dog, Grace, has learned to identify subtle changes in my behavior that precede anxiety episodes with an accuracy that sometimes startles me. When she detects these early warning signs, she's trained to perform specific interruption behaviors: a firm nudge with her nose, positioning herself to make physical contact, or gently taking my hand in her mouth to redirect my attention. These interventions often prevent full panic attacks from developing or significantly reduce their intensity by breaking the escalation cycle before it reaches the point of no return.

During acute episodes, Grace is trained to provide deep pressure therapy by lying across my lap or chest, creating a calming physical sensation that helps regulate my nervous system. This intervention draws on research showing that deep pressure stimulation can activate the parasympathetic nervous system, promoting relaxation and reducing the intensity of panic responses. The weight and warmth of the dog offer both physical comfort and a grounding sensation that helps interrupt the dissociative aspects of severe panic attacks.

She also positions herself between me and other people, creating a protective buffer that reduces the feeling of being trapped or overwhelmed that often accompanies panic attacks. This behavior, known as "blocking" or "covering," serves multiple functions: it creates physical space that reduces sensory input, provides a psychological barrier that enhances feelings of safety, and signals to others that the handler needs space without requiring verbal communication during a crisis.

The effectiveness of these interventions extends beyond immediate crisis management. Over time, handlers often develop increased confidence in their ability to manage anxiety because they know their dog will provide early warning and intervention support. This confidence can reduce the anticipatory anxiety that often perpetuates panic disorder, creating a positive feedback loop that enhances overall mental health stability.

Medication Retrieval and Reminder Services

Many people with mental health conditions take medications that must be accessed quickly during episodes or taken on strict schedules for optimal effectiveness. Psychiatric service dogs can be trained to retrieve medication bottles on command, bring water for taking medications, or provide timed medication reminders. While this task might seem straightforward compared to other types of service dog work, its impact on medication compliance and crisis management can be profound.

Medication retrieval training typically starts with basic fetch commands and evolves into specific protocols for locating, retrieving, and delivering medications safely. Dogs learn to differentiate between medication containers, respond to urgency cues from their handlers, and complete retrieval tasks even when their handlers are experiencing severe symptoms that impair movement or clear communication.

This task becomes especially crucial during severe depressive episodes, when basic self-care can feel overwhelming, or during dissociative episodes, when cognitive function may be temporarily impaired. Having a dog trained to retrieve necessary medications can mean the difference between managing an episode successfully and requiring emergency intervention.

Service dogs can also be trained to provide medication reminders at specific times for individuals on strict medication schedules. This might involve bringing the medication container to the handler, performing specific alert behaviors at set times, or activating alarm systems to ensure medications aren't forgotten during periods of cognitive impairment or distraction.

Beyond the practical benefits of medication access, these tasks often provide psychological support by reducing anxiety around medication management. Handlers report feeling more confident in managing their conditions independently, knowing their dog can assist with medication access during crises or times of impaired functioning.

Nightmare Interruption and Sleep Assistance

PTSD-related nightmares can be particularly devastating, not just because of the immediate distress they cause, but because the fear of recurring nightmares often leads to chronic insomnia and avoidance of sleep altogether. This creates a vicious cycle: sleep deprivation worsens PTSD symptoms, which in turn increases the frequency and intensity of nightmares, further disrupting sleep patterns.

Psychiatric service dogs can be trained to recognize signs of nightmare distress—changes in breathing, movement, or vocalizations that occur during sleep—and to wake their handler using specific, gentle techniques that minimize disorientation and panic upon waking. This intervention requires sophisticated training that teaches dogs to distinguish between regular sleep movements and distress indicators, and to respond with the appropriate level of intensity and technique.

Nightmare interruption training typically involves teaching dogs to recognize specific sleep disturbance patterns and respond with graduated interventions. This might begin with gentle nudging or licking, escalate to more persistent physical contact, and ultimately include turning on lights or leading the handler to a different location if initial efforts are insufficient to interrupt the nightmare.

Some dogs are trained to turn on lights, create physical space from the handler to prevent accidental injury during a startled awakening, or lead the handler to another room to help break the cycle of nightmare-related anxiety. The goal is not simply to wake the handler, but to do so in a way that minimizes trauma and supports a return to restful sleep.

The impact of effective nightmare interruption extends far beyond the immediate relief of being awakened from a distressing dream. Handlers report improved sleep quality, reduced anxiety about going to sleep, and decreased overall PTSD symptom severity when their sleep is protected by trained intervention. Knowing that their dog will interrupt nightmares before they become overwhelming often allows handlers to sleep more deeply and consistently.

Environmental Assessment and Safety Tasks

For individuals with PTSD, anxiety disorders, or certain autism spectrum presentations, entering new or crowded environments can trigger significant distress. The hypervigilance that characterizes many anxiety and trauma-related conditions creates constant scanning for potential threats, leading to exhaustion and avoidance of new environments. Service dogs can be trained to perform room searches, checking corners, closets, or other areas where the handler feels vulnerable, providing reassurance that the space is safe.

This task draws on dogs' natural investigative abilities while channeling them into specific protocols that address human anxiety patterns. Dogs learn to systematically check environments according to their handler's specific concerns, returning with clear signals that indicate whether the space has been assessed and found safe.

Grace performs what we call "room clearing"—systematically checking a new environment and returning to me with a specific signal that indicates the area has been assessed. This task directly addresses the hypervigilance symptoms of PTSD while allowing me to enter new spaces with greater confidence. Rather than spending mental energy scanning for threats, I can rely on Grace's assessment and focus on the purpose of my visit to the new environment.

The training for environmental assessment involves teaching dogs to search specific areas on command, investigate potential hiding spots or areas of concern, and return to their handler with clear communication about their findings. Dogs learn to differentiate between normal environmental features and potential concerns, though the goal is typically reassurance rather than actual threat detection.

Some dogs are also trained to find exits in unfamiliar buildings, providing their handlers with immediate knowledge of escape routes that can reduce anxiety in crowded or enclosed spaces. This task combines environmental assessment with practical safety preparation, addressing both the psychological need for escape route awareness and the practical benefit of emergency preparedness.

Grounding and Reality Orientation

Dissociation—feeling disconnected from one's body, surroundings, or sense of reality—is a common symptom of trauma-related disorders, severe anxiety, and other mental health conditions. During dissociative episodes, individuals may feel as though they are observing their lives from outside their bodies, lose awareness of their physical surroundings, or experience changes in their perception of time and reality.

Service dogs can be trained to provide grounding assistance through specific physical contact, guided movement, or tasks that help orient handlers to their environment and reconnect with their immediate physical reality. These interventions work by offering sensory input that anchors the handler in the present environment and physical experience.

This might involve the dog providing firm, consistent physical pressure to help the handler reconnect with their body, guiding them to a specific location, or performing repetitive behaviors that help reestablish the handler's connection to their environment.

Some dogs are trained to carry out specific tactile interventions, such as applying pressure to certain parts of the handler's body, providing deep pressure therapy, or engaging in repetitive physical contact that supports sensory awareness. Others learn to guide their handlers through particular movements or to specific locations that aid in restoring environmental awareness.

Social Buffer and Crowd Navigation

For individuals with anxiety disorders, autism spectrum conditions, or PTSD, crowded environments can trigger overwhelming symptoms related to sensory overload, social anxiety, or trauma responses. The combination of multiple stimuli, unpredictable movement patterns, and social demands can quickly escalate anxiety to unmanageable levels.

Service dogs can be trained to create physical space around their handler, position themselves as barriers between their handler and others, or guide their handler to less crowded areas. These tasks require sophisticated training that teaches dogs to assess crowd density, recognize handler distress signals, and respond with appropriate spatial management interventions.

Grace has learned to position herself strategically in lines, create space in crowded elevators, and guide me toward less populated areas when she senses my anxiety escalating. Her interventions are subtle enough not to draw unwanted attention while providing enough space and buffering to keep my anxiety manageable.

These tasks aren't about avoiding all social situations—they're about making social participation possible by reducing the overwhelming aspects of crowd interaction. The goal is to enable handlers to engage in community activities, work environments, and social gatherings that might otherwise be too overwhelming to manage successfully.

The Science Behind the Bond

The effectiveness of psychiatric service dogs isn't just anecdotal— research continues to demonstrate measurable improvements in various outcomes for handlers. While the field is still developing and more research is needed, existing studies provide compelling evidence of the therapeutic value of well-trained psychiatric service dogs across multiple domains of functioning.

Physiological Changes

Studies have documented reductions in cortisol levels (a stress hormone), lower heart rate and blood pressure during stressful situations, and improved sleep patterns among psychiatric service dog handlers. The presence of a trained service dog appears to have measurable effects on the body's stress response systems, suggesting that the benefits extend beyond psychological comfort to include physiological regulation.

Research on the human-animal bond has shown that interaction with dogs can trigger the release of oxytocin, often called the "bonding hormone," while simultaneously reducing cortisol production. For psychiatric service dog handlers, these physiological changes may be amplified by the constant presence of their working partner and the dog's specific training to respond to stress signals.

Cardiovascular benefits observed in service dog handlers include not only acute stress reduction during episodes but also improvements in baseline stress indicators over time. This suggests that the presence of a psychiatric service dog may help regulate the stress response system overall, rather than simply providing temporary relief during crises.

Improvements in sleep among psychiatric service dog handlers include both increased duration and better quality. These changes may result from several factors, including nightmare interruption, heightened feelings of safety and security, and the routine and structure that come with caring for a dog.

Functional Improvements

Research consistently shows improvements in daily functioning among service dog handlers, including increased ability to complete routine tasks, greater independence in community activities, and reduced reliance on emergency mental health services. These are not just quality-of-life enhancements—they represent measurable changes in functional capacity that can be documented and tracked over time.

Studies measuring activities of daily living report significant improvements in handlers' ability to manage routine tasks such as grocery shopping, attending appointments, and maintaining employment. These gains appear to result from both the specific task assistance that service dogs provide and the increased confidence and reduced anxiety that handlers experience with their working partners.

Measures of community participation show increased engagement in social activities, volunteer work, and community organizations among psychiatric service dog handlers. This greater involvement often develops gradually as handlers gain confidence in managing their symptoms with their dog's assistance and become more comfortable navigating public spaces.

Employment outcomes among psychiatric service dog handlers indicate improvements in job retention, success with workplace accommodations, and career advancement. These outcomes may stem from better symptom management, greater confidence in requesting and using accommodations, and the specific support service dogs can offer in work settings.

Healthcare utilization patterns show reductions in emergency mental health services, psychiatric hospitalizations, and crisis interventions among psychiatric service dog handlers. These changes suggest that service dogs may help with crisis prevention and management, reducing the need for more intensive and costly care.

Social Integration Benefits

Perhaps surprisingly, service dogs often serve as social facilitators, making it easier for handlers to engage in community activities, maintain employment, and sustain relationships. The dog provides a conversation starter and a source of confidence, enabling greater social participation.

Research on social outcomes for psychiatric service dog handlers documents improvements in relationship quality, family functioning, and community engagement. These improvements appear to result from multiple factors, including reduced social anxiety, increased confidence in managing symptoms in social situations, and the social facilitation that often occurs around service dogs.

Many handlers report that their service dogs act as "social lubricants," making it easier to initiate conversations and connect with others in community settings. While this social attention can sometimes be overwhelming, many handlers learn to manage these interactions in ways that enhance, rather than hinder, their social engagement.

The presence of a service dog often signals to others that accommodation and understanding may be needed, potentially reducing the stigma and misunderstanding that individuals with invisible disabilities often face. This can lead to more supportive social interactions and reduced stress about disclosure and accommodation requests.

Family relationship improvements documented among psychiatric service dog handlers include better communication, reduced caregiver burden, and improved family functioning. Family members often report feeling less anxious about their loved one's safety and independence when a trained service dog is present to provide assistance and crisis intervention.

Service Dogs as Treatment Complements, Not Replacements

One of the most crucial aspects of psychiatric service dog partnerships that prospective handlers must understand is how these animals function within the broader context of mental health treatment. Despite the profound benefits these partnerships can provide, service dogs are never intended to replace traditional mental health care—rather, they serve as sophisticated assistive technology that can enhance a person's ability to implement therapeutic strategies and participate more fully in their recovery process.

The Evidence for Integrated Care

Research consistently demonstrates that the most successful psychiatric service dog partnerships occur when the dogs are integrated into comprehensive treatment plans that include ongoing therapy, appropriate medication management, and other evidence-based interventions. A study published in the Journal of Consulting and Clinical Psychology found that veterans with PTSD who received psychiatric service dogs while continuing their existing mental health treatment showed significantly greater improvements in symptoms and quality of life measures compared to those who relied solely on traditional treatment or those who discontinued professional care after receiving their dogs.[34]

The Department of Veterans Affairs, while not yet providing psychiatric service dogs directly, has begun studying how these partnerships affect treatment outcomes for veterans enrolled in their mental health programs. Preliminary findings suggest that veterans who acquire service dogs through reputable programs while maintaining their VA mental health care show improved medication compliance, increased therapy attendance, and reduced utilization of crisis services.[35]

How Service Dogs Enhance Traditional Treatment

Service dog tasks often provide practical support that enables handlers to implement coping strategies learned in therapy more effectively. For individuals learning grounding techniques in cognitive behavioral therapy, a service dog trained to provide deep pressure therapy during panic attacks offers immediate, reliable access to a calming intervention that might otherwise be difficult to implement during acute episodes.

Individuals with psychiatric service dogs, including veterans with posttraumatic stress disorder (PTSD), have been shown to report increased engagement with therapeutic activities, such as entering challenging environments and participating in social situations, compared to those without service dogs. Multiple studies indicate that the presence of a highly trained service dog may function as a psychological safety net, facilitating greater confidence in practicing coping skills and contributing to enhanced quality of life. This effect is particularly notable when service dog placement is integrated with ongoing mental health care and therapy.[35] (Leighton et al., 2024; O'Haire & Rodriguez, 2018).

Coordination Between Treatment Teams

Successful integration requires communication between handlers, their mental health providers, and service dog training organizations. Many reputable training programs now encourage or require ongoing mental health treatment throughout the application and training process, recognizing that the most successful partnerships develop when multiple forms of support work together.

K9 Partners for Patriots, for example, maintains relationships with mental health professionals who can provide consultation during the training process and ongoing support after placement. Program director feedback suggests that handlers who continue therapy while training with their dogs show better long-term outcomes than those who view the service dog as a replacement for professional care.

Some mental health providers have begun incorporating service dog partnerships into treatment planning, helping clients identify how their dog's trained tasks align with therapeutic goals and how to maximize the benefits of both interventions. This coordination helps ensure that the service dog's presence enhances rather than interferes with therapeutic progress.

When Service Dogs May Complicate Treatment

While integration generally improves outcomes, mental health professionals have identified scenarios where service dog partnerships might inadvertently interfere with treatment goals. Some individuals may become overly dependent on their dogs, using the animal's presence to avoid addressing underlying issues that require therapeutic work.

It is important to recognize that service dogs are not a replacement for evidence-based mental health treatment. Some clinicians have noted that, on occasion, handlers may become overly dependent on their dogs and forgo the necessary therapeutic practices that foster long-term recovery. Maintaining active engagement in therapy and self-management skills, alongside service dog support, leads to the most sustainable progress.

Other potential complications include handlers who discontinue medication against medical advice after receiving their service dogs, believing the animal's support eliminates the need for pharmaceutical intervention. Research consistently shows that while service dogs can improve quality of life and functional capacity, they do not address the underlying neurochemical imbalances that many psychiatric medications target.

Some handlers may also struggle with the increased social attention that comes with having a service dog, particularly if social anxiety is a significant component of their condition. This visibility can temporarily worsen symptoms before handlers adapt to managing public interactions more effectively.

Measuring Outcomes in Integrated Treatment

Mental health providers who work with service dog handlers report using various measures to assess how the partnership affects treatment progress. Standardized assessments like the PTSD Checklist for DSM-5 (PCL-5) or the Generalized Anxiety Disorder 7-item scale (GAD-7) can track symptom changes over time, while functional measures assess improvements in daily living activities, social participation, and occupational functioning.

Through my work with health care professionals, I've learned that some individuals can become overly dependent on their dogs in ways that actually interfere with recovery. I've met handlers who've said things like, "I don't need to practice those breathing techniques my therapist taught me because my dog handles my anxiety for me," or "Why should I work on exposure therapy when my dog makes me feel safe?"

This represents a fundamental misunderstanding of how service dogs should function within recovery. Grace doesn't eliminate my need to develop coping skills—she provides a safety net that makes it possible for me to practice those skills in challenging situations. Her alert to rising anxiety gives me the opportunity to implement the grounding techniques I learned in therapy before my symptoms become overwhelming.

The most successful partnerships I've observed are those where handlers view their service dogs as sophisticated tools that enhance their ability to engage in therapeutic work, not replace it. The dog's support should make you feel confident enough to tackle challenging therapeutic goals, not provide an excuse to avoid them

Some providers track specific metrics like therapy attendance rates, medication compliance, emergency service utilization, and self-reported confidence in managing symptoms. These objective measures help distinguish between the genuine improvements service dogs provide and the temporary euphoria that sometimes accompanies new interventions.

The Role of Ongoing Mental Health Support

Long-term success in psychiatric service dog partnerships often depends on maintaining access to mental health support throughout the dog's working career. Life circumstances change, mental health conditions may fluctuate, and the challenges of service dog partnership itself may require professional guidance to navigate successfully.

Handlers who maintain relationships with mental health providers report greater confidence in managing both their mental health conditions and the complexities of service dog partnership. They have professional support for processing the emotional challenges of increased visibility, navigating workplace accommodations, and eventually managing the transition when their service dog retires.

The retirement transition, in particular, often benefits from professional mental health support. As handlers face returning to previous levels of limitation while grieving the loss of their working partner, ongoing therapy can provide essential coping resources and help maintain the progress achieved during the partnership.

Research on Combined Treatment Approaches

Emerging research suggests that the combination of psychiatric service dogs with traditional mental health treatment may be more effective than either intervention alone. A longitudinal study following PTSD patients found that those who received service dogs while continuing therapy and medication management showed significantly greater improvements in sleep quality, social functioning, and overall symptom severity compared to control groups receiving only traditional treatment[34,35].

While no large-scale studies have yet examined this question specifically in individuals with severe anxiety disorders, both research and clinical consensus emphasize the value of integrating service dog partnerships into broader mental health treatment. Studies in PTSD and related conditions suggest that the most stable and successful long-term outcomes occur when service dog handlers continue to participate in regular professional care—such as therapy and medication management—after receiving their dogs, rather than viewing the dog as a replacement for clinical support. Leading service dog organizations and mental health professionals recommend ongoing engagement in treatment, noting that this combined approach supports greater symptom stability, functional improvement, and reduces the risk of setback or relapse

Building Effective Treatment Teams

The most successful psychiatric service dog partnerships often involve treatment teams that include the handler, mental health professionals, service dog trainers, and sometimes family members or other support persons. This collaborative approach ensures that all aspects of the handler's recovery are coordinated and mutually reinforcing.

Regular communication between team members helps identify potential problems early and ensures that the service dog's role remains appropriate within the broader treatment context. It also provides opportunities to adjust both therapeutic approaches and service dog tasks as the handler's needs evolve over time.

Understanding psychiatric service dogs as sophisticated treatment adjuncts rather than standalone solutions helps set appropriate expectations and maximizes the potential benefits these partnerships can provide. When integrated thoughtfully into comprehensive treatment plans, service dogs can significantly enhance recovery outcomes while supporting handlers in developing the skills and confidence needed for long-term mental health stability.

CHAPTER 3

Protected Partnerships: Understanding Your Legal Rights

Americans with Disabilities Act: Your Foundation of Rights

Understanding your legal rights as a psychiatric service dog handler isn't just academic knowledge; it's practical information that determines your access to employment, housing, public accommodation, and community participation. The legal framework can seem complex, but grasping the key principles empowers you to advocate effectively for yourself and navigate situations where your rights might be challenged.

> "Understanding your rights isn't academic knowledge—it determines your access to employment, housing, and community participation."

The Americans with Disabilities Act is one of the most comprehensive civil rights laws in U.S. history, fundamentally reshaping how society accommodates individuals with disabilities. For psychiatric service dog handlers, the ADA provides the legal foundation for independence and community participation. Yet many handlers, and even more members of the general public, remain unaware of the specific protections and limitations that govern service dog access rights.

The complexity of ADA law often leads to confusion and conflict in real-world situations. Business owners may be uncertain about their obligations, resulting in inappropriate denial of access or excessive questioning. Handlers may be unsure of their rights, leading to acceptance of unlawful discrimination or a failure to advocate for appropriate accommodation. Understanding the specific provisions and practical applications of ADA law is essential for both handlers and the communities they live in.

The power of legal rights lies not just in their existence but in their use. A right that isn't understood or exercised offers no protection. For psychiatric service dog handlers, whose disabilities are often invisible and whose dogs' tasks may not be immediately apparent to others, legal knowledge is particularly crucial to ensure equal access and fair treatment in all aspects of community life.

Title II: State and Local Government Services

Title II of the ADA covers all services, programs, and activities of state and local governments. This means your psychiatric service dog has access rights to public transportation systems, government buildings, courthouses, public schools and universities, libraries, parks, and any other facility operated by state or local government entities.

The scope of Title II protection extends to virtually every interaction individuals have with government services. This includes not only obvious government buildings like city halls and courthouses but also public universities, community colleges, public hospitals, public housing authorities, public transportation systems, and even government-sponsored events and programs.

The practical implications are significant and affect daily life in numerous ways. Your service dog can accompany you to jury duty, where the stress of legal proceedings might otherwise trigger anxiety or PTSD symptoms that could interfere with civic participation. City council meetings, school board meetings, and other public forums for civic engagement must accommodate your service dog, ensuring that your disability doesn't prevent you from participating in democratic processes.

Public college classes represent another crucial area of Title II protection. Students with psychiatric service dogs have the right to bring their dogs to lectures, seminars, laboratories, and other educational activities. This protection extends beyond classroom attendance to include dormitory living, campus dining facilities, student activities, and all other aspects of university life.

DMV appointments, passport offices, social services offices, and other government service locations must accommodate psychiatric service dogs, recognizing that the stress of bureaucratic processes can be particularly challenging for individuals with anxiety disorders, PTSD, or other mental health conditions. The support service dogs provide in these environments often means the difference between successfully completing necessary tasks and avoidance that can lead to legal or practical complications.

Public transportation systems—buses, trains, subways—must accommodate your service dog without additional fees or restrictions beyond those that apply to all passengers. This protection is especially crucial for psychiatric service dog handlers who may depend on public transportation to access employment, healthcare, education, and community resources.

This protection also extends to public housing authorities and any housing programs administered by government entities. If you live in public housing or receive housing assistance through government programs, your psychiatric service dog is protected regardless of pet policies or breed restrictions that might otherwise apply.

Title III: Public Accommodation

Title III covers businesses and organizations that serve the public, including restaurants, hotels, retail stores, medical facilities, entertainment venues, and service establishments. With very limited exceptions, these entities must allow your psychiatric service dog to accompany you wherever customers are normally allowed to go.

The breadth of Title III coverage encompasses virtually every aspect of commercial and public life. Restaurants, from fast-food spots to fine dining venues, must accommodate psychiatric service dogs in all customer seating areas. The anxiety reduction and PTSD symptom management that service dogs provide often make dining out possible for individuals who might otherwise avoid restaurants due to crowded environments, unpredictable social interactions, or trauma-related triggers.

This means restaurants cannot require you to sit in a specific section because you have a service dog. The practice of segregating service dog teams to back corners, near kitchen doors, or in less desirable seating areas violates ADA requirements and perpetuates the discrimination the law was designed to eliminate.

Hotels cannot charge pet deposits or cleaning fees for your service dog, recognizing that service dogs are medical equipment rather than pets. This protection extends to all aspects of hotel accommodations, including room selection, amenity access, and use of common areas.

Stores cannot prohibit your service dog from entering, even if they have "no pets" policies. This includes grocery stores, department stores, pharmacies, banks, and all other retail establishments. The independence that grocery shopping represents becomes possible when service dogs can accompany their handlers into these essential community resources.

Movie theaters, concert venues, and sporting events must accommodate your service dog without additional charges. Entertainment and recreational activities play important roles in mental health maintenance and social connection.

Medical facilities, from doctors' offices to hospitals, must accommodate psychiatric service dogs, with limited exceptions for sterile environments.

This protection is especially important for psychiatric service dog handlers, who may experience significant anxiety about medical appointments or procedures.

The key limitation is that your service dog must be under your control and housebroken. If your dog is disruptive—barking excessively, being aggressive, or not responding to your commands—businesses have the right to ask you to remove the animal. However, they must still provide you with their services if possible, even without the dog present.

This limitation requires a careful balance between accommodation rights and legitimate business interests. The behavior standards applied to service dogs must be reasonable and based on actual disruption, not assumptions about what constitutes appropriate behavior.

What Questions Can Be Asked?

This is one of the most practical aspects of ADA law for daily life. Under federal law, when it's not apparent that your dog is a service animal, staff at businesses or government facilities can ask only two specific questions: [4]

1. "Is this dog a service animal required because of a disability?"
2. "What work or task has this dog been trained to perform?"

These two questions' limitations represent a careful balance between legitimate verification needs and privacy protection for individuals with disabilities. The questions are designed to confirm that the animal meets the legal definition of a service animal without requiring disclosure of specific medical information or disability details.

They cannot ask about your specific disability, require documentation or certification, ask for a demonstration of the trained task, or charge fees because of the service dog's presence. These prohibitions protect handler privacy while preventing the creation of bureaucratic barriers that could effectively deny access through administrative burden.

RED FLAG: Any business demanding "papers" or certification is violating federal law.

REMEMBER: Only two questions allowed: "Is this a service dog?" and "What task is it trained for?"

The prohibition against asking about specific disabilities recognizes that disability disclosure is a personal choice and should not be required for public accommodation. Many psychiatric conditions carry stigma that could lead to discrimination if disclosure were mandated.

The prohibition against requiring documentation reflects a deliberate decision to avoid creating a registration or certification system that could become a barrier to access. Unlike some countries that require official documentation for service animals, the U.S. system relies on self-identification combined with the two permissible questions to verify service animal status.

They cannot ask these questions if it is obvious the dog is a service animal—for example, if the dog is clearly guiding someone who is blind. This provision recognizes that some service dog work is immediately apparent, making verification questions unnecessary and potentially intrusive.

For psychiatric service dog handlers, whose disabilities and dogs' tasks are often invisible to observers, the verification questions are more likely to be asked. This reality makes it particularly important for handlers to understand their rights and prepare appropriate responses.

Understanding these limitations protects you from inappropriate questioning while helping you prepare effective responses. When asked about trained tasks, you can be specific without providing exhaustive detail. Responses like "She's trained to interrupt panic attacks and guide me to exits during anxiety episodes" provide sufficient information without oversharing personal medical details.

Preparing appropriate responses serves multiple purposes beyond simple compliance. Clear, confident replies often end questioning quickly and professionally, reducing stress and confrontation.

The tone and manner of questioning can be as important as the content. Staff members who ask verification questions in hostile, suspicious, or challenging tones create discriminatory environments even when asking legally permissible questions. Handlers have the right to expect that verification questions be asked respectfully and professionally.

Section 504 of the Rehabilitation Act

Section 504 extends ADA-like protections to any program or activity that receives federal funding. This includes most schools, universities, hospitals, and many social service organizations. For psychiatric service dog handlers, this means expanded access to educational and healthcare settings that might not otherwise be covered under ADA provisions.

The scope of Section 504 is often broader than Title II of the ADA because it covers private entities that receive federal funding, not just government agencies. This distinction is particularly important in healthcare and education, where many private institutions receive federal funding through grants, contracts, student financial aid, or other federal programs.

In educational settings, this protection is especially important. Students with psychiatric service dogs have the right to attend classes, live in dormitories, and participate in school activities with their service animals. Schools cannot charge additional fees or deposits, though they may require proof of current vaccinations and evidence that the dog is housebroken.

The educational support that psychiatric service dogs provide can be essential for academic success. Students with PTSD may need their service dogs to perform room searches in new classrooms, provide grounding during flashbacks, or interrupt nightmares in dormitory settings. Students with severe anxiety may require their dogs to provide deep pressure therapy during exams, guide them to exits during panic attacks, or create social buffers in crowded campus environments.

Healthcare facilities receiving federal funding must accommodate psychiatric service dogs, with limited exceptions for sterile environments where the dog's presence could compromise medical procedures. The key is that accommodation must be made wherever possible, and alternative arrangements should be offered when the service dog cannot be present.

When service dogs cannot be present in specific medical settings—such as operating rooms or certain imaging procedures—healthcare facilities must offer alternative accommodations. This might include allowing the dog to remain nearby until the last possible moment, providing sedation or anxiety medication to help the handler cope without their dog, or scheduling procedures at times that minimize the separation period.

Fair Housing Act Protections

Housing protections for service dog handlers extend beyond what's available for pet owners or even emotional support animal handlers. Under the Fair Housing Act, service dogs are not considered pets, which means pet policies, pet deposits, and breed restrictions don't apply to them.[5]

The Fair Housing Act provides some of the strongest protections available to psychiatric service dog handlers, recognizing that stable housing is fundamental to mental health recovery and that service dogs are essential medical equipment rather than lifestyle choices.

This protection covers virtually all housing situations—rental apartments, condominiums, housing cooperatives, and most single-family home rentals. Even housing with strict "no pets" policies must accommodate service dogs. Landlords cannot charge pet deposits, monthly pet fees, or require additional insurance coverage because of your service dog.

The protection also extends to breed restrictions. Even if your housing has policies prohibiting certain breeds, your psychiatric service dog is protected regardless of breed. This is particularly important given that some effective service dog breeds—German Shepherds, Rottweilers, or pit bull mixes—are often subject to breed discrimination in housing.

However, you remain responsible for any damage your service dog causes beyond normal wear and tear, and the dog must not pose a direct threat to other residents. Housing providers can still enforce lease terms related to noise complaints or disruptive behavior, but these standards must be applied equally to all residents.

The damage responsibility provision ensures that service dog accommodations don't create unfair financial burdens for housing providers while maintaining the principle that handlers are responsible for their animals' behavior.

The direct threat provision requires individual assessment based on actual behavior, not assumptions about particular breeds or disabilities. Determining that a service dog poses a direct threat must be based on objective evidence of dangerous behavior that cannot be eliminated through reasonable modifications to policies or procedures.

Workplace Accommodation

While the ADA doesn't automatically guarantee that psychiatric service dogs can accompany handlers to all workplaces, it does require employers to consider service dog accommodation as part of the reasonable accommodation process under Title I of the ADA.

The workplace accommodation analysis differs significantly from public accommodation requirements because employers must balance accommodation requests with legitimate business needs, safety requirements, and potential impacts on other employees or customers. Despite these complexities, many handlers successfully negotiate workplace accommodations that allow their psychiatric service dogs to accompany them to work.

The key is demonstrating that the service dog's presence addresses work-related limitations caused by your disability and that the accommodation would not create undue hardship for the employer.

This might involve providing separate office space, modifying work schedules to accommodate the dog's needs, or creating protocols for the dog's presence in meetings or customer interactions.

Office space modifications might include private offices for handlers whose service dogs may be distracting in open work environments, designated dog exercise and relief areas during work hours, or protocols for dog care during meetings or travel.

Work schedule modifications might include flexibility for dog care needs, time for service dog training appointments, or arrangements for dog coverage during business travel.

Exceptions and Limitations

Understanding where service dog access rights do not apply helps prevent conflicts and prepares you for situations where alternative arrangements may be necessary. These narrowly defined exceptions must be based on legitimate, objective criteria rather than assumptions or stereotypes about disabilities or service dogs.

Religious Organizations

Churches, temples, mosques, and other houses of worship operated by religious organizations are exempt from ADA public accommodation requirements. This means religious organizations can set their own policies regarding service dogs, though many choose to accommodate them voluntarily.

The religious organization exemption reflects the constitutional principle of religious freedom and the recognition that religious institutions must be able to operate according to their beliefs and practices. However, this exemption applies only to religious functions and activities, not to secular activities that religious organizations may sponsor.

Many religious organizations voluntarily accommodate service dogs, recognizing that inclusion and accessibility align with their spiritual values of compassion and community.

Private Clubs

Truly private clubs that do not serve the general public are exempt from ADA requirements. However, many facilities that appear to be private clubs serve the public in ways that make them subject to ADA requirements.

The distinction between truly private clubs and public accommodations often depends on factors such as membership criteria, public advertising, and the extent to which the facility serves non-members.

Sterile Environments

Operating rooms, burn units, intensive care units, and other sterile medical environments may exclude service dogs when their presence would compromise medical care. However, alternative accommodations should be provided when possible.

The sterile environment exception applies only when the service dog's presence would create actual health or safety risks that cannot be eliminated through reasonable modifications.

When service dogs cannot be present in sterile environments, healthcare facilities must offer alternative accommodations to minimize the impact on the handler.

Direct Threat

Access can be denied if your service dog poses a direct threat to other people or property that cannot be eliminated through reasonable modifications. However, this determination must be based on an actual assessment of the specific dog's behavior, not on assumptions based on breed or disability type.

The direct threat standard requires objective evidence of dangerous behavior that creates a significant risk of substantial harm to others. This standard cannot be met through speculation, assumptions about particular breeds, or fear based on appearance.

The assessment of direct threat must consider the nature, duration, and severity of the risk, the probability that potential harm will occur, and whether reasonable modifications can eliminate or reduce the risk.

When direct threat determinations are made, they should be documented with specific behavioral observations and explained to the handler. Handlers who believe they have been subjected to improper direct threat exclusions have recourse through administrative complaints and legal action.

The legal framework protecting psychiatric service dog handlers represents a comprehensive system that ensures equal access and participation in all aspects of community life. Understanding these rights and their limitations empowers handlers to advocate effectively for themselves while helping communities create truly inclusive environments where people with disabilities can thrive.

CHAPTER 4

Training Programs and Success Rates

The Statistical Reality: Understanding Success Rates and Challenges

Before exploring the inspiring stories of successful service dog partnerships, it's essential to understand the statistical realities that shape this field. These numbers aren't meant to discourage anyone from pursuing a psychiatric service dog but rather to set realistic expectations and help individuals make informed decisions about this significant commitment.

The world of service dog training operates under statistical constraints that many prospective handlers find surprising or even discouraging. The romanticized image of service dogs often portrayed in the media suggests that most dogs can be trained for this work with enough effort and dedication. The reality is far more complex and demanding, involving rigorous selection criteria, intensive training protocols, and substantial failure rates even among carefully chosen candidates.

Understanding these statistical realities serves multiple purposes beyond simple expectation management. For prospective handlers, it helps explain why professional training programs are expensive, why waiting lists are long, and why the process demands such significant time and resource commitments. For families considering a service dog, it provides context for making informed decisions about whether to invest in professional training, attempt owner-training, or explore alternative accommodation strategies.

The statistics also highlight why fraudulent service dog claims are so problematic for the legitimate community. When genuine service dog training sees substantial failure rates even among carefully selected candidates, the presence of untrained pets presented as service dogs undermines public understanding of what legitimate service dog work truly involves.

Most importantly, understanding these realities helps prospective handlers approach service dog pursuit with appropriate preparation, realistic timelines, and backup plans in case their particular situation does not lead to a successful partnership. This preparation often makes the difference between a devastating disappointment and a learning experience that leads to alternative solutions.

Candidate Selection Success Rates

The often-cited (perhaps more anecdotal than factual) statistic that only about 1% of randomly selected dogs would qualify for service dog training programs reflects the rigorous requirements these animals must meet. Service dogs need a specific combination of temperament, intelligence, physical health, and trainability that simply isn't present in most dogs, regardless of breed or background.

This statistic becomes more meaningful when understood in the context of what service dog work actually requires. Unlike pet dogs, who need only basic obedience and socialization to live successfully with human families, service dogs must perform complex tasks reliably in unpredictable environments while maintaining perfect public behavior under all circumstances. They must work consistently regardless of distractions, stress, illness, or environmental changes that would excuse poor behavior in pet dogs.

"Only about 1% of randomly selected dogs would qualify for service dog training programs."

Successful service dog candidates must demonstrate calm confidence in new environments, the ability to focus despite distractions, stable temperament under stress, strong motivation to work with humans, and the physical stamina to perform their duties for 8–10 years. They must be neither overly aggressive nor overly timid, must have strong problem-solving abilities, and must be able to generalize their training to new situations.

The temperament requirements alone eliminate the vast majority of dogs from consideration for service work. Dogs that are too reactive to environmental stimuli cannot maintain focus on their handler's needs in busy public environments. Dogs that are too independent may not maintain the close attention to human cues that service work requires. Dogs that are too sensitive may become overwhelmed by the stress of constant public access and task performance.

Physical health requirements further narrow the candidate pool. Service dogs must have sound joint structure to withstand years of public access work, stable digestive systems that function reliably despite stress or schedule changes, and sensory capabilities that enable them to detect subtle changes in their handler's condition. Dogs with chronic health issues, genetic predispositions to common disorders, or physical limitations that could interfere with task performance cannot safely or effectively serve as working animals.

The intelligence and trainability requirements eliminate dogs that cannot learn complex task sequences, cannot reliably generalize training to new environments, or cannot maintain learned behaviors over time without constant reinforcement. Service dog work requires dogs that can learn quickly, retain training consistently, and adapt their responses to changing circumstances while maintaining reliability.

Professional training programs invest considerable resources in careful candidate selection precisely because the stakes are so high. A service dog that doesn't perform reliably isn't just an expensive disappointment; it can be dangerous for a handler who depends on the animal's trained responses for daily functioning and safety.

The selection process typically involves multiple phases of evaluation, beginning with basic temperament testing and progressing through increasingly complex assessments of working ability, stress tolerance, and task aptitude. Dogs that pass initial screening may still be eliminated during later phases if they cannot maintain performance standards under more demanding conditions.

Many programs maintain their own breeding stock specifically to increase the likelihood of producing suitable candidates. Even with careful genetic selection and early development protocols designed to optimize working potential, these programs still experience substantial candidate failure rates, highlighting the inherent challenges of producing reliable working animals.

Training Success Rates

Even among dogs selected specifically for service work, success rates vary significantly based on training approach and program quality. Professional training programs accredited by organizations like Assistance Dogs International report varying success rates, though specific figures should be verified with individual organizations.[11] Success rates can vary widely depending on the population served, the dogs' source, and the type of training. There is no single, universally reported success rate for all ADI-accredited programs.

The variation in success rates among professional programs reflects the complexity of service dog training and the multiple variables influencing outcomes. Programs with more rigorous candidate selection may report higher training success rates but also eliminate more dogs during initial screening. Programs that accept more marginal candidates may have lower training success rates but provide opportunities for dogs that other programs would reject.

Training methodology significantly impacts success rates, with programs using positive reinforcement techniques generally reporting better outcomes than those relying on correction-based methods.

However, even within positive training approaches, variations in timing, consistency, and trainer expertise create differences in program effectiveness.

The reasons for training failure vary widely and often occur despite careful candidate selection and professional training expertise. Some dogs develop medical issues that prevent them from working, such as joint problems, making mobility assistance painful; digestive issues causing unpredictable bathroom needs; or sensory changes interfering with task performance.

Others exhibit behavioral changes as they mature, making them unsuitable for service work. Adolescent dogs may develop reactivity that is not apparent during puppy evaluation, or adult dogs may lose motivation for work as their personalities stabilize. Some dogs that show excellent promise during initial training cannot maintain performance standards when exposed to the full complexity of real-world service environments.

Some simply lack the sustained motivation required for the intensive training process, while others cannot reliably generalize their training to real-world situations. Dogs that perform perfectly in controlled training environments may become unreliable when exposed to the unpredictability of actual public access work. Others may learn specific tasks well but cannot adapt their responses to variations in environment, timing, or handler needs.

The washout process itself requires careful management to ensure dogs transition appropriately when training cannot continue. Dogs that don't complete service training aren't failures; many go on to become beloved family pets, therapy animals, or working dogs in other capacities. Understanding these realities helps explain why professionally trained service dogs are expensive and why waiting lists are often substantial.

The timing of training failures varies significantly, with some dogs washing out during early socialization phases and others completing most of their training before elimination during final public access testing. Late-stage washouts are particularly costly for training programs and emotionally difficult for handlers, who may have begun developing relationships with dogs that ultimately cannot serve them.

Owner-Training Considerations

For individuals who choose to train their own service dogs, success rates are generally lower than those of professional programs, particularly for first-time handlers. Success varies widely based on the handler's experience, access to professional guidance, and the dog's individual characteristics. Success rates improve significantly for those who collaborate with professional trainers while retaining primary responsibility for their dog's training.

The appeal of owner-training is understandable, particularly for individuals with limited financial resources or those living in areas without access to professional programs. Owner-training also offers the potential for creating exceptionally strong bonds between handler and dog, enhancing the dog's ability to read subtle changes in the handler's condition.

The challenges of owner-training are significant and often underestimated by prospective handlers. Most people lack experience with advanced dog training techniques, do not have access to controlled training environments, and may struggle to maintain the emotional objectivity needed to assess their dog's suitability for service work. Additionally, the bond between owner and dog, while valuable, can sometimes interfere with the training process if the dog becomes overly protective or dependent.

The absence of professional training expertise becomes particularly problematic during complex phases of service dog development. Public access training requires exposure to environments and situations that may be difficult for handlers to access or control. Task training often requires precise timing and techniques that inexperienced trainers may not recognize or implement correctly.

The emotional challenges of owner-training often prove more difficult than the technical aspects. Making objective assessments about a beloved pet's suitability for service work requires a level of detachment many owners find impossible to maintain. Recognizing when training isn't progressing successfully and making decisions about whether to continue often conflicts with the emotional investment developed during training.

However, owner-training offers distinct advantages, particularly for psychiatric service dogs. The intense bonding that occurs during training can enhance the dog's sensitivity to subtle changes in the handler's emotional or physiological state. The handler gains intimate knowledge of the dog's capabilities and limitations, which is valuable for ongoing care and training maintenance.

The flexibility of owner-training allows handlers to adapt training protocols to their specific needs, disabilities, and circumstances in ways standardized programs may not accommodate. Handlers can focus on tasks that address their particular functional limitations, spending less time on skills that are less relevant to their situations.

Owner-training also provides greater control over timing and pacing, enabling handlers to adjust training intensity based on their mental health status, work schedules, and family obligations. This flexibility can be especially valuable for individuals with psychiatric conditions that fluctuate in severity or create periods when intensive training activities are not feasible.

Understanding Service Dogs in Training

During the months or years it takes to develop a service dog, these animals fall into a special category known as "service dogs in training" or SDiTs. Understanding this phase helps clarify both the training process and the public interactions that prospective handlers and trainers may encounter during this time.

Legal Status and Public Access Rights

Service dogs in training occupy a unique legal position that varies significantly by state. Unlike fully trained service dogs, which have comprehensive access rights under federal ADA law, SDiTs' access rights are determined by individual state legislation. Some states grant broad public access rights to dogs in training when accompanied by approved trainers, while others offer no special protections beyond those given to pets.

This variation in state laws creates confusion for both trainers and the public. In states with SDiT access laws, dogs in training may be permitted in public accommodations, restaurants, and transportation systems, but only when accompanied by approved trainers or puppy raisers who meet specific state requirements. These laws typically require that the handler be affiliated with a recognized training organization and that the dog exhibit appropriate public behavior.

However, it's important to understand that SDiT access rights, where they exist, apply only during legitimate training activities conducted by approved organizations or individuals. These protections do not extend to pet owners attempting to train their own dogs without professional guidance, nor do they apply to dogs that are not enrolled in formal service dog training programs.

The Training Progression

The SDiT phase represents the visible portion of service dog development occurring in public settings. During this period, dogs learn essential public access skills while developing the confidence and focus necessary for service work. This training typically progresses through several distinct phases, each building on previous learning.

Early socialization involves exposing young dogs to a variety of environments, people, and situations they'll encounter throughout their working lives. Trainers take SDiTs to grocery stores, restaurants, shopping malls, airports, and other public venues to practice appropriate behavior around distractions. During this phase, dogs learn basic impulse control, how to ignore food on the floor, how to remain calm around other people and animals, and how to focus on their handler despite environmental stimuli.

As training progresses, SDiTs learn more complex skills such as proper positioning in crowded spaces, appropriate responses to elevator rides, and calm behavior during transportation. They practice walking through crowds without pulling or becoming overstimulated, settling quietly under restaurant tables, and maintaining attention on their trainer despite interesting sights, sounds, and smells.

Advanced training phases involve task-specific education that varies based on the type of service work the dog will eventually perform. For psychiatric service dogs, this might include early versions of interruption behaviors, basic alert training, or preliminary work on crowd navigation and environmental assessment.

Public Interaction During Training

SDiTs in public often attract significant attention from curious observers who may not understand that these dogs are working and learning. Well-meaning people frequently want to pet, talk to, or feed dogs in training, not realizing that these interactions can interfere with critical learning processes.

Professional trainers typically outfit SDiTs with special vests or patches that identify them as dogs in training and request that the public not interact with them. However, these identifiers aren't legally required and don't carry the same weight as the protections afforded to fully trained service dogs. Trainers must be prepared to educate the public on why distraction-free training is essential for the dog's development.

The behavior standards for SDiTs are necessarily lower than those expected of fully trained service dogs, but they should still demonstrate appropriate public manners. Dogs in training may have occasional accidents, might require more direction from their handlers, or could become overwhelmed in challenging environments. However, they should not be aggressive, excessively disruptive, or completely out of control.

Training Environment Challenges

The SDiT phase presents unique challenges for both dogs and trainers. Dogs must learn to work in unpredictable public environments while still developing the skills and confidence that will eventually make them reliable service animals. Trainers must balance the dog's learning needs with public accommodation requirements and social expectations.

Weather conditions, crowd levels, and environmental factors can all affect training sessions in ways that controlled indoor environments cannot replicate. A dog might perform perfectly in a training facility but become overwhelmed in a busy airport or confused by the sounds and movements in a crowded restaurant. These real-world challenges are essential for building the adaptability and confidence that working service dogs need.

The unpredictability of public training environments also means trainers must be highly skilled in reading their dogs' stress levels and knowing when to modify or end training sessions. Pushing a dog beyond its current capabilities can create negative associations with public environments that may affect its future working ability.

Owner-Training Considerations

For individuals pursuing owner-training approaches, the SDiT phase becomes particularly complex. Owner-trainers typically do not have the same public access rights that professional programs enjoy, limiting their ability to practice essential skills in real-world environments.

This limitation often requires owner-trainers to become creative about finding suitable training opportunities. They might practice in pet-friendly businesses, seek permission from sympathetic business owners, or focus heavily on private property training before gradually introducing more challenging public environments once their dogs have developed sufficient skills.

The owner-training approach also requires individuals to become experts in canine behavior and training techniques while simultaneously managing their own disabilities. This dual challenge makes the SDiT phase especially demanding for owner-trainers, who must learn to read their dogs' behavior and respond appropriately while also addressing their own symptom management needs.

Timeline and Expectations

The SDiT phase typically lasts anywhere from six months to two years, depending on the training approach, the individual dog's learning pace, and the complexity of tasks being taught. This extended timeline requires patience from prospective handlers who are eager to have their working partner fully trained and available.

During this period, dogs are not yet reliable enough to provide the consistent support that handlers ultimately need. The SDiT may perform tasks correctly in some situations but fail in others, or may require more handler guidance than a fully trained service dog. Understanding these limitations helps set appropriate expectations for the training process.

The transition from SDiT to a fully trained service dog isn't marked by a specific ceremony or certification, but instead represents the point at which the dog consistently demonstrates reliable task performance and appropriate public behavior across a wide variety of environments and situations.

Distinguishing Legitimate Training

The SDiT designation is sometimes misused by individuals seeking public access for pets not genuinely enrolled in service dog training programs. Legitimate SDiTs should be accompanied by trainers who can explain the dog's training program, demonstrate the dog's current skill level, and provide information about the organization overseeing the dog's development.

Real training programs maintain detailed records of each dog's progress, follow established curricula, and work toward specific behavioral and task performance goals. Training should be systematic, progressive, and focused on developing the specific skills service dogs require for public access and task performance.

Understanding the SDiT phase helps illustrate both the complexity of service dog development and the significant time investment required to create reliable working animals. It also encourages public awareness about why these dogs in training deserve respectful space to learn the skills they'll need throughout their working careers.

Professional Training Programs: Two Primary Approaches

The landscape of professional service dog training has evolved to include two distinct philosophical approaches, each reflecting different theories about optimal training methodology and handler preparation. Understanding these approaches helps prospective handlers make informed decisions about which type of program may best meet their needs and circumstances.

Traditional Program Model

The conventional approach involves organizations maintaining complete control over all training phases until the final handler matching and placement. This model has dominated service dog training for decades and continues to represent the majority of established programs, particularly those that serve individuals with physical disabilities.

Program Selection Criteria

Reputable service dog training programs should provide clear information about their success rates, training methods, follow-up support, and accreditation status. Programs accredited by Assistance Dogs International or similar organizations have met specific standards for training quality, handler support, and ongoing service.

The accreditation process involves rigorous evaluation of training protocols, facility standards, handler support services, and outcome measurement. Programs seeking accreditation must demonstrate consistent success rates, appropriate follow-up services, and ethical treatment of both animals and handlers. Accreditation provides prospective handlers assurance that programs meet professional standards and industry best practices.

Be cautious of programs guaranteeing specific timelines, promising unrealistic success rates, or pressuring you to make immediate financial commitments. Legitimate programs typically have waiting lists and thorough application processes involving medical documentation, interviews, and sometimes home visits.

The application process itself provides insight into program quality and approach. Reputable programs invest significant time in handler evaluation to ensure appropriate matches between dogs and handlers. This evaluation typically assesses the handler's disability-related needs, living situation, support systems, and ability to maintain a working dog throughout its career.

Programs accepting applications without thorough evaluation or promising immediate placement often lack the depth of training and support required for successful partnerships. The complexity of service dog training and the individualized nature of disability accommodation make quick placements nearly impossible for legitimate programs maintaining appropriate standards.

Traditional Training Timeline and Process

Traditional service dog training typically takes anywhere from 6-24 months, though this can vary based on the specific tasks being trained, the individual dog's learning pace and the training model. The process generally includes several distinct phases that build upon each other to create reliable working animals.

Early puppy development focuses on socialization, basic obedience, and temperament evaluation. During this phase, which typically lasts 4-6 months, trainers assess the dog's suitability for continued training while building foundational skills required for all service dogs. This period involves extensive exposure to various environments, people, animals, and situations the dog will encounter throughout its working life.

The socialization process goes far beyond what pet dogs typically receive, involving systematic exposure to specific stimuli service dogs must handle calmly. This includes crowded public spaces, unusual sounds and surfaces, medical equipment, transportation systems, and interactions with people of all ages and abilities. The goal is to develop dogs that remain calm and focused regardless of environmental challenges.

Task-specific training follows, where dogs learn particular skills they'll need to assist their eventual handler. For psychiatric service dogs, this might include panic attack interruption, medication retrieval, crowd navigation, or nightmare interruption. This phase typically lasts 8-12 months and requires consistent, professional-level training expertise.

The task training phase represents the most technically demanding aspect of service dog development. Trainers must teach complex behavioral sequences, ensure reliable performance under varying conditions, and maintain task quality while building the dog's confidence and motivation. The precision required for effective task performance often demands training expertise that takes years to develop.

Handler training represents the final phase, where the prospective handler learns to work effectively with their new service dog. This isn't just about learning commands; it involves understanding the dog's communication signals, maintaining training consistency, and integrating the dog's assistance into daily routines. Handler training typically requires several weeks of intensive work, often followed by months of ongoing support and periodic check-ins.

The handler training phase often proves more challenging than anticipated, requiring handlers to learn not only specific commands but also timing, body language, and communication techniques that enable an effective partnership. Many handlers find that working with a pre-trained dog requires significant adjustment to their own behavior and expectations.

Community-Based Training Model

An alternative approach, exemplified by organizations like K9 Partners for Patriots, uses a community-based model where the handler and dog are trained together from the beginning. Rather than pre-training a dog and then matching it with a handler, this model focuses on training the handler to train their dog.

This approach reflects a different philosophy about the nature of service dog partnerships and the skills handlers need for long-term success. Instead of viewing handlers as recipients of pre-trained animals, the community-based model treats them as active participants in their dog's development and ongoing training maintenance.

Community-Based Timeline and Process

Community-based programs typically involve 6 to 9 months of weekly training classes where handlers learn both basic dog training principles and specific psychiatric service dog task development. The timeline is generally shorter than traditional programs because the handler is actively involved in all phases of training rather than receiving a pre-trained dog.

The compressed timeline reflects the efficiency gained when handlers and dogs learn together from the beginning. Rather than requiring separate phases for dog training and handler education, the community-based model integrates these processes, allowing simultaneous development of both partners' skills.

However, training doesn't end after the formal class period. Since handlers are taught the principles and techniques of ongoing training, they continue developing their dogs' skills long after the structured program concludes. This approach creates handlers who can adapt their dog's training to changing needs and maintain skills throughout the dog's working life.

The ongoing development aspect is one of the key advantages of community-based training. Handlers who understand training principles can modify tasks as their needs change, add new skills as circumstances require, and maintain training quality throughout their dog's career. This adaptability is often valuable for psychiatric service dog handlers, whose needs may fluctuate based on changes in mental health status or life circumstances.

Ongoing Support and Services

Organizations using the community-based model often provide comprehensive, ongoing support that extends well beyond basic dog training. K9 Partners for Patriots, for example, offers lifetime support to veterans, including mental health counseling, continued training assistance, and community support services. This holistic approach recognizes that successful service dog partnerships require attention to both the handler's mental health needs and the ongoing development of the dog's skills.

The support services offered by community-based programs often address the broader context of disability and recovery rather than focusing solely on the service dog partnership. This might include connections to mental health resources, help with navigating disability benefits, career counseling, or family support services that reflect the interconnected nature of mental health recovery.

The community aspect of these programs fosters peer support networks that can be especially valuable for veterans or others who may feel isolated by their disabilities. Handlers who train together often maintain relationships that offer ongoing encouragement, practical advice, and social connection—supporting both mental health recovery and successful service dog partnerships.

Comparing the Two Approaches

Both models offer distinct advantages that may make them more suitable for different handlers or circumstances. Traditional programs provide dogs with extensive foundational training and may be appropriate for handlers who prefer to receive a dog with established skills. The community-based model fosters handlers who deeply understand their dog's training and can continue skill development throughout the partnership.

The choice between approaches often depends on individual preferences, geographic availability, and specific needs. Some handlers thrive with the hands-on involvement of community-based training, while others prefer the structure and established protocols of traditional programs.

Handlers with limited time for intensive training, who lack confidence in learning dog training skills, or who prefer the assurance of receiving a fully trained animal may find traditional programs more suitable. These programs also offer extensive quality control through professional training and evaluation, which can result in more consistent outcomes. However, even in highly reputable programs, some handler-dog matches do not succeed, and ongoing support remains critical.

Handlers who want to be actively involved in their dog's development, have the time and motivation for ongoing training, or need the flexibility to adapt training to changing circumstances may find community-based programs more appealing. These programs often provide stronger ongoing support networks and more comprehensive services that address the broader context of disability and recovery.

Geographic availability frequently influences program choice, as traditional programs may be located far from prospective handlers, while community-based programs often have more flexible location options. Cost structures may also differ, with some community-based programs offering more affordable options for handlers with limited financial resources.

Financial Investment and Funding Options

The frequently cited cost range of $15,000–$30,000[16,17] for professionally trained service dogs reflects the substantial resources required for successful programs. This includes puppy acquisition and early care, professional trainer salaries, facility costs, veterinary care, and ongoing support services. However, fees may vary depending on the organization, location, and services provided. Some programs offer dogs at little or no cost to recipients, subsidized by fundraising or grants.

> **TRUTH:** Professional training takes 6-24 months and costs $15,000-$30,000. There are no shortcuts.

Understanding the cost structure helps explain why service dog training is expensive and why programs require significant time and resource commitments. The cost breakdown typically includes several major categories that reflect the complexity and duration of service dog development.

Puppy acquisition and early care costs include breeding or purchase expenses, veterinary care, vaccinations, and early socialization activities. Programs that maintain their own breeding stock incur additional expenses for breeding animal care, genetic testing, and breeding program management.

Professional trainer salaries represent a significant portion of program costs, reflecting the specialized expertise required for service dog training. Experienced service dog trainers command higher salaries than general dog trainers due to the technical complexity of their work and its legal implications.

Facility costs include training spaces, equipment, vehicle expenses for public access training, and administrative overhead. Many programs require specialized facilities that can accommodate multiple dogs, training equipment, and public access practice environments.

Veterinary care expenses include routine healthcare, emergency treatment, and specialized medical evaluations that may be required during training. Working dogs often require more extensive veterinary care than pets because of the physical demands of their work and the need to maintain optimal health throughout their careers.

Many programs serving veterans offer services at no cost to qualified recipients, funded through donations, grants, and fundraising activities. Organizations like K9s for Warriors,[7] Pups4Patriots,[8] and numerous smaller regional programs specifically serve veterans with service-related mental health conditions.

Veteran programs typically receive funding from various sources, including private donations, corporate sponsorships, foundation grants, and government contracts. Some programs receive partial funding through Veterans Administration benefits or other government programs, though direct federal funding for service dog training remains limited.

For non-veterans, funding options are more limited but do exist. Some programs offer sliding scale fees based on income, payment plans, or partial scholarships. Others fundraise specifically for individual placements, helping handlers raise funds through community support.

Individual fundraising has become increasingly common as crowdfunding platforms and social media have made it easier to reach potential donors. Many handlers successfully raise funds through GoFundMe campaigns, community events, and local business sponsorships, though this approach requires significant time and effort.

Some insurance companies are beginning to cover service dog costs, particularly for handlers with documented mental health conditions and clear medical necessity. However, insurance coverage remains inconsistent and often requires extensive documentation and appeals processes.

Owner-Training: A Viable but Challenging Path

The decision to pursue owner-training represents a significant commitment, offering both substantial advantages and considerable challenges. Understanding both aspects helps prospective handlers make informed decisions about whether this approach aligns with their capabilities, resources, and circumstances.

Advantages of Owner-Training

Owner-training can create exceptionally strong bonds between handler and dog, potentially enhancing the animal's ability to detect subtle changes in the handler's condition. The handler gains comprehensive knowledge of the dog's training, capabilities, and limitations, which can be valuable for ongoing maintenance and problem-solving.

The bonding that occurs during intensive training often results in partnerships uniquely attuned to each other's needs and communication styles. Handlers who train their own dogs often report that their animals seem to anticipate their needs and respond to subtle cues that might not be apparent to dogs trained by others.

Owner-training also offers greater flexibility in terms of timing, specific task selection, and training methods. Handlers can adapt the training process to their specific needs and circumstances rather than fitting into a program's standardized approach.

This flexibility becomes particularly valuable for handlers with psychiatric conditions that may fluctuate in severity or create periods when intensive training activities are not feasible. Owner-trainers can adjust training schedules, intensity, and methods based on their current mental health status and available resources.

The cost savings of owner-training can be substantial, though the process often requires significant time investments instead of financial outlays. Handlers who successfully owner-train may spend thousands rather than tens of thousands of dollars, though professional consultation and training materials still represent meaningful expenses.

Realistic Assessment of Challenges

However, owner-training requires substantial time, dedication, and often a financial investment in professional guidance. Most successful owner-trainers work with professional service dog trainers, at least periodically, to ensure proper technique and objective assessment of progress.

The time commitment for owner-training often exceeds what prospective handlers anticipate. Effective service dog training requires daily practice sessions, regular public access outings, and consistent reinforcement of learned behaviors. This commitment must continue for months or years and often competes with work, family, and health management responsibilities.

The emotional attachment between owner and dog can sometimes interfere with objective evaluation. It's difficult to make the decision to "wash out" a beloved pet when training isn't progressing successfully, even when continuing may not be in anyone's best interest.

This emotional challenge often proves more difficult than the technical aspects of training. Recognizing when a cherished companion lacks the temperament or ability for service work requires a level of objectivity that emotional bonds can compromise. Many owner-trainers continue training long past the point when professional programs would have made washout decisions.

The lack of professional expertise can lead to training errors that are difficult to correct later in the process. Inappropriate timing, inconsistent methods, or inadequate socialization during critical developmental periods can create problems that persist throughout the dog's career.

Professional Support for Owner-Trainers

Successful owner-training almost always involves some level of professional guidance. This might include an initial temperament evaluation, periodic training consultations, public access test preparation, or troubleshooting specific challenges that arise during training.

Many professional trainers offer owner-training support services, providing guidance while allowing the handler to maintain primary responsibility for their dog's development. This approach combines the benefits of professional expertise with the advantages of owner-training.

The investment in professional consultation often determines the success or failure of owner-training efforts. Handlers who attempt to train without any professional guidance typically experience lower success rates and may inadvertently create behavioral problems that require extensive correction later.

Maintaining Training: The Ongoing Commitment

The relationship between a service dog and the handler doesn't end when initial training is completed. Instead, it represents the beginning of a lifelong partnership that requires ongoing maintenance, adaptation, and development throughout the dog's working career.

Training Doesn't End at Placement

Whether a service dog is professionally trained or owner-trained, the partnership requires ongoing maintenance throughout the dog's working life. Service dogs need regular refresher training, continued socialization, and adaptation to changes in their handler's life.

This ongoing commitment includes daily training practice, regular veterinary care, appropriate exercise and mental stimulation, and periodic professional evaluations to ensure the dog's skills remain sharp and reliable.

The daily practice requirements often surprise new handlers who may assume that a trained service dog will maintain its skills automatically. Like any learned behavior, service dog tasks require regular reinforcement to maintain reliability and precision.

Recognizing When Help is Needed

Successful service dog handlers learn to recognize when their dog's performance is declining or when new challenges require additional training. This might include behavioral changes due to aging, new medical conditions that affect the dog's work, or changes in the handler's needs that call for additional task training.

Professional support should be sought whenever training issues arise that can't be resolved through routine practice. Early intervention often prevents minor issues from becoming serious problems that could compromise the partnership.

One of the most important skills handlers must develop is the ability to recognize when professional help is needed. Pride, financial constraints, or attachment to the current partnership can sometimes prevent handlers from seeking help when problems arise, leading to deterioration in the working relationship that might have been avoided with timely intervention.

These statistical realities—the rigorous selection criteria, intensive training protocols, and substantial failure rates—underscore why legitimate service dog training demands such significant investments of time, expertise, and resources. But understanding the numbers is only part of the story. To truly appreciate why these partnerships can be so transformative when they work, and why the training process is so demanding, it's essential to look beneath the surface at the sophisticated science that creates reliable, life-changing partnerships between handlers and their psychiatric service dogs. The remarkable capabilities that Grace and dogs like her demonstrate daily aren't accidents or simple obedience—they're the result of carefully applied learning theory, precise behavior shaping, and an understanding of both human psychology and canine cognition that transforms well-intentioned pets into working medical equipment.

CHAPTER 5

The Science Behind Service Dog Training

Understanding What Lies Beneath: An Introduction to Training Science

This section provides an educational overview of how psychiatric service dogs are trained to perform the specific tasks that transform them from well-behaved pets into working medical equipment. This is not a training guide—excellent, comprehensive training manuals are available for those pursuing that path. Instead, the goal is to help readers understand the scientific principles and methodical processes that create reliable, life-changing partnerships between handlers and their psychiatric service dogs.

Understanding how training works serves multiple purposes for a diverse readership. Mental health professionals gain insight into the sophistication and reliability of service dog interventions, helping them better support clients considering or working with service dogs. Educators learn about accommodation tools that can support students with mental health conditions in academic settings. Community leaders develop an appreciation for the complexity behind what may appear to be simple animal companionship, informing policy decisions and public education efforts. Prospective handlers formulate realistic expectations about the complexity and time investment required for successful partnerships. Family members and support networks gain a clearer understanding of what their loved ones are undertaking when they pursue service dog partnerships.

The training of psychiatric service dogs combines centuries-old principles of animal learning with modern understanding of both canine cognition and human psychology. Unlike training pet dogs for basic obedience, service dog training must create behaviors that are reliable under stress, consistent across environments, and responsive to subtle human cues that may not be apparent to observers.

This scientific approach distinguishes legitimate service dog training from the superficial "training" that produces fake service dogs wearing purchased vests. Real service dog training involves the systematic application of learning theory, careful behavior shaping, extensive generalization practice, and ongoing maintenance throughout the dog's working life. The investment of time, expertise, and resources required for this level of training helps explain both why legitimate service dogs are expensive and why they are so effective.

Understanding these training principles also clarifies why psychiatric service dogs represent genuine medical accommodations rather than lifestyle choices or emotional support preferences. The specific, trained responses these dogs provide address measurable functional limitations in ways that can be documented, evaluated, and relied upon for daily independence and safety.

The Science of Learning: Classical and Operant Conditioning in Service Dog Training

Service dog training relies on two fundamental principles of learning theory that work together to create complex, reliable behaviors: classical conditioning and operant conditioning. Understanding these principles illuminates how trainers can teach dogs to recognize subtle changes in human behavior and respond with specific, helpful interventions. For psychiatric service dogs, this science becomes particularly sophisticated because they must detect and respond to internal human experiences that often have minimal external signs.

Classical Conditioning in Psychiatric Service Dogs

Classical conditioning, first described by Ivan Pavlov, creates associations between stimuli that allow dogs to predict and respond to events before they fully develop. In psychiatric service dog training, classical conditioning enables dogs to associate early warning signs of mental health episodes with the need to perform specific tasks.

The Remarkable Science of Canine Detection

The foundation of psychiatric service dog effectiveness lies in dogs' extraordinary sensory capabilities. Research indicates that a dog's sense of smell is estimated to be 10,000 to 100,000 times more sensitive than that of humans, with some estimates reaching up to 1 million times more sensitive.[31] This remarkable olfactory capability becomes the cornerstone of their ability to detect the physiological changes that accompany mental health episodes.

When humans experience anxiety, panic, or other stress responses, our bodies release hormones, including adrenaline and cortisol. These chemical changes create subtle alterations in our scent that trained dogs can learn to recognize with remarkable precision. What makes this particularly valuable for psychiatric service dog work is that these chemical changes often occur before we become consciously aware of escalating symptoms—sometimes 15 to 45 minutes before we recognize the developing episode ourselves.

Grace's ability to alert me to rising anxiety before I'm aware of it stems from this biological reality. Her brain processes chemical information that mine cannot detect, creating an early warning system that allows intervention before symptoms become overwhelming. This isn't mystical intuition—it's sophisticated biological detection combined with learned behavioral responses.

> **KEY FACT:** Dogs detect stress chemicals 15-45 minutes before you're consciously aware of rising anxiety.

Beyond Scent: The Complexity of Behavioral Recognition

While scent detection forms the foundation, psychiatric service dogs also learn to recognize subtle behavioral patterns that precede episodes. Grace has learned to identify my specific pre-anxiety indicators: changes in my breathing rhythm, particular postures I adopt when stress is building, or repetitive behaviors like nail-biting that signal escalating symptoms.

This behavioral pattern recognition represents a different type of learning—one that requires dogs to observe, categorize, and respond to human behavior with remarkable consistency. Unlike scent detection, which relies on biological capabilities dogs naturally possess, behavioral recognition must be systematically developed through extensive exposure and reinforcement.

The sophistication becomes apparent when you consider that Grace must distinguish between normal variations in my behavior and patterns that indicate a genuine need for intervention. She must recognize the difference between casual nail-biting and the obsessive nail-biting that signals rising anxiety, or between normal breathing changes and the specific patterns that precede panic episodes.

Operant Conditioning in Task Performance

Operant conditioning, developed by B.F. Skinner focuses on how consequences shape behavior. In service dog training, operant conditioning teaches dogs that performing specific tasks in response to handler cues or detected changes results in positive outcomes, making them more likely to repeat those behaviors reliably.

The Precision Required for Psychiatric Work

The operant conditioning that creates Grace's panic attack interruption demonstrates the remarkable precision required for psychiatric service dog work. When she detects my escalating anxiety, she doesn't simply approach me—she performs a specific sequence of behaviors calibrated to be maximally helpful without being overwhelming.

Her response involves particular types of physical contact, applied with specific pressure and maintained for optimal duration. This isn't accidental; it's the result of learning theory principles that shaped her responses to be as therapeutic as possible. She has learned that certain types of contact are more effective than others, that timing matters enormously, and that her own emotional state affects the quality of support she can provide.

The deep pressure therapy Grace provides during panic attacks illustrates another sophisticated application of operant conditioning. She has learned to position herself to provide calming pressure while remaining alert to my changing needs. If the pressure becomes uncomfortable, she adjusts. If I need to move, she accommodates while maintaining supportive contact. These nuanced responses represent complex behavioral repertoires developed through systematic reinforcement of helpful actions.

The Challenge of Invisible Disabilities

What makes psychiatric service dog training particularly demanding is that these dogs must respond to internal human experiences that may not have obvious external manifestations. Unlike guide dogs that navigate visible obstacles or seizure alert dogs that respond to dramatic physical changes, psychiatric service dogs must detect and respond to conditions that may be largely invisible to human observers.

This invisibility creates unique training challenges. Dogs must learn to recognize and respond to experiences like dissociation, flashbacks, or panic attacks that may have subtle or highly variable external signs. The reliability required for this work—where a missed alert could result in a handler becoming overwhelmed in public or avoiding necessary activities—demands training approaches that account for this complexity.

The Neuroscience Behind the Partnership

Recent research has begun to illuminate why psychiatric service dog partnerships are particularly effective from a neurobiological perspective. When humans and dogs interact positively, both species experience increases in oxytocin—often called the "bonding hormone"—while simultaneously experiencing decreases in cortisol production.

For psychiatric service dog handlers, these physiological changes may be amplified by the constant presence and reliable support the dog provides. The knowledge that trained intervention is available can reduce anticipatory anxiety, while the physical contact involved in many psychiatric service dog tasks can activate parasympathetic nervous system responses that promote relaxation and emotional regulation.

This neurobiological foundation helps explain why the human-canine bond in service dog partnerships often becomes so profound. The relationship isn't just emotional; it's physiologically reinforcing for both species, creating powerful incentives for continued cooperation and mutual support.

The Integration of Multiple Systems

Perhaps most remarkably, sophisticated psychiatric service dogs learn to integrate multiple detection and response systems simultaneously. Grace monitors my scent for chemical changes, observes my behavior for warning patterns, and remains aware of environmental factors that might affect my stress levels—all while maintaining the public access behaviors required for her to accompany me into community settings.

This multi-layered capability represents the culmination of both species' remarkable abilities: canine sensory and learning capabilities combined with human understanding of mental health needs and training science. The result is partnerships that can provide support with precision and reliability that often surpasses what handlers could achieve independently or through other interventions.

Understanding this scientific foundation helps explain why legitimate service dog training requires such significant investments of time, expertise, and resources. The behavioral repertoires these dogs develop represent sophisticated applications of learning science, combined with careful attention to the unique challenges of psychiatric disability accommodation.

The science also illuminates why these partnerships often become so transformative. They're not just about having a well-trained animal; they're about accessing biological capabilities and learned responses that can detect and address human needs with remarkable sensitivity and consistency. For individuals whose mental health conditions create functional limitations, this level of support can mean the difference between isolation and community participation, between crisis management and confident independence.

Alerting Tasks: Early Detection and Prevention

Alerting tasks represent some of the most sophisticated aspects of psychiatric service dog training. They require dogs to recognize subtle changes in their handler's condition and respond with specific behaviors that provide early warnings of developing episodes.

Physiological Detection and Scent Work

Dogs possess extraordinary sensory capabilities that enable them to detect physiological changes associated with mental health episodes. Their sense of smell, estimated to be anywhere from 10,000 to a million times more sensitive than that of humans, allows them to detect chemical changes during stress responses.

Training dogs to recognize these scent changes involves systematic exposure to samples collected during different emotional states, paired with specific reward protocols that teach the dog to alert when they detect the target scents. This process requires careful attention to timing and consistency to ensure the dog learns to discriminate between normal scent variations and those indicating developing episodes.

Behavioral Pattern Recognition

Beyond scent detection, psychiatric service dogs can be trained to recognize subtle behavioral patterns that precede mental health episodes. These might include changes in movement, posture, breathing, or repetitive behaviors that indicate rising anxiety or developing episodes.

For me, Grace has learned to recognize behaviors such as when I start rocking in my chair or biting my nails obsessively—signs that my anxiety is escalating before I'm fully aware of the change. When she observes these warning signs, she responds with specific alerting behaviors: nudging my leg or positioning herself in my lap to provide grounding contact.

Training for behavioral pattern recognition involves careful observation during the handler's daily life to identify consistent warning signs, followed by systematic training to teach the dog to respond to those specific behaviors. This requires extensive practice in various environments to ensure the dog can recognize the patterns regardless of context or distractions.

Alert Response Training

Once dogs learn to recognize warning signs, they must be trained to respond with specific alerting behaviors that effectively communicate with their handlers. These alert responses must be distinctive enough to get the handler's attention while remaining appropriate for public environments.

Common alert responses include specific types of nudging, positioning behaviors, or bringing particular items to the handler. The key is teaching the dog to perform these responses consistently and only in response to the specific warning signs they've been trained to recognize.

Grace's alerting behavior involves nudging my leg or positioning herself in my lap when she detects early signs of my anxiety. This physical contact serves multiple purposes: it gets my attention, provides immediate grounding through pressure and warmth, and gives me a clear signal to implement my coping strategies before the anxiety escalates further.

Interruption Tasks: Breaking Cycles and Providing Grounding

Interruption tasks address episodes that are already in progress, requiring dogs to recognize acute symptoms and respond with behaviors that help break destructive cycles or provide a stabilizing influence during crises.

Nightmare Interruption Training

Nightmare interruption represents one of the most sophisticated interruption tasks, requiring dogs to recognize signs of sleep disturbance and respond with gentle waking techniques that minimize disorientation and panic upon awakening.

Grace's nightmare interruption training taught her to recognize when I'm experiencing distress during sleep—talking loudly, thrashing, or moaning that indicates nightmares or night terrors. Although she usually sleeps in her kennel in my room, she learned to come out when she detects these signs, approach the bed, and gently lick my face until I wake up.

The training process for nightmare interruption typically begins with teaching the dog to recognize specific sounds or movements that indicate sleep disturbance. This might involve playing recordings of distress sounds or using other training aids that allow practice without requiring the handler to actually experience nightmares during training sessions.

The dog must learn to differentiate between normal sleep movements and sounds versus those indicating distress. This discrimination training requires careful attention to the specific indicators that characterize problematic episodes as opposed to normal sleep patterns.

The waking technique itself requires delicate training to ensure the dog provides enough stimulation to wake the handler without causing startlement or injury. Grace learned to use gentle, persistent licking rather than sudden movements or sounds that might increase disorientation upon waking.

Follow-through training teaches the dog to continue providing support after the initial waking. Grace has learned to follow me if I need to walk around the house to reset after a nightmare, and she stays in bed with me until I fall back asleep before returning to her kennel. This extended support helps ensure complete recovery from the episode.

Panic Attack Interruption

When panic attacks are already in progress, interruption tasks focus on breaking the escalation cycle and providing grounding assistance that helps handlers regain control over their symptoms.

During my panic attacks, Grace provides interruption through physical contact—licking my leg, positioning herself in my lap, or applying pressure with her body weight. These behaviors work by redirecting my attention from internal panic symptoms to external sensory input, helping ground me in the present moment.

Training for panic attack interruption involves teaching dogs to recognize the signs of acute episodes and respond with specific calming behaviors. The dog must learn to approach handlers who may be agitated or disoriented and provide comfort without becoming overwhelmed by the handler's distress.

The pressure and warmth Grace provides during panic attacks serve multiple physiological functions. Deep pressure stimulation can activate the parasympathetic nervous system, promoting relaxation and reducing the intensity of panic responses. The physical contact also offers sensory grounding that helps interrupt the dissociative aspects of panic episodes.

Repetitive Behavior Interruption

For individuals with autism, OCD, or other conditions involving repetitive or self-injurious behaviors, psychiatric service dogs can be trained to recognize these patterns and provide gentle interruptions that redirect attention to more adaptive behaviors.

This training involves teaching dogs to identify specific repetitive behaviors and respond with alternative actions that engage the handler's attention. The interruption must be gentle and consistent, rather than startling or punitive, helping redirect behavior without creating additional stress.

Task-Specific Training for Different Conditions

Different mental health conditions require specialized training approaches that address the unique functional limitations and symptoms associated with each diagnosis.

PTSD-Specific Training Applications

PTSD symptoms create specific training opportunities that address hypervigilance, environmental concerns, and trauma-related triggers. Dogs can be trained to perform room searches that provide reassurance about space safety, allowing handlers to enter new environments with greater confidence.

Training for room searching involves teaching dogs to systematically check areas of concern—corners, closets, behind doors—and return to their handler with clear signals indicating the space has been assessed. This task directly addresses hypervigilance symptoms while providing practical safety information.

Environmental awareness training teaches dogs to position themselves strategically in public spaces, creating physical barriers between their handlers and potential triggers. This might involve blocking crowded aisles, positioning at the handler's back in restaurants, or creating space in elevators and other confined areas.

Depression and Motivation Support

Depression-related training focuses on tasks that provide structure, motivation, and routine support during periods when basic self-care becomes challenging. Dogs can be trained to provide medication reminders, encourage movement and activity, and interrupt harmful or self-destructive behaviors.

Medication reminder training involves teaching dogs to retrieve specific medication containers at designated times or in response to handler cues. This task becomes particularly valuable during severe depressive episodes, when cognitive function may be impaired and routine self-care feels overwhelming.

Activity encouragement training teaches dogs to engage their handlers in movement and interaction during periods of withdrawal or inactivity. This might involve bringing specific items that encourage activity, providing persistent but gentle interaction to motivate engagement, or performing behaviors that require handler response and movement.

Autism Spectrum Applications

Autism-related training addresses sensory regulation, social navigation, and safety concerns unique to autism spectrum presentations. Dogs can be trained to provide deep pressure therapy during sensory overload, interrupt stimming behaviors that might be harmful, and assist with safety for individuals who may wander or fail to recognize environmental dangers.

Sensory regulation training teaches dogs to recognize signs of sensory overload and respond with specific calming interventions. This might include providing pressure therapy, guiding the handler to quieter environments, or performing repetitive behaviors that help regulate the handler's sensory system.

Social buffer training teaches dogs to create physical space in crowded environments, position themselves between their handler and overwhelming social stimuli, and provide confidence support during social interactions that might otherwise be too challenging to navigate successfully.

The Training Process: From Foundation to Specialization

Understanding the progression from basic training to specialized task work illustrates the systematic approach required for successful psychiatric service dog development.

Foundation Training

All service dog training begins with extensive foundation work that includes basic obedience, public access skills, and socialization. This foundation builds the behavioral stability and environmental confidence needed for more advanced task training.

Public access training ensures dogs can behave appropriately in all environments where they may accompany their handlers. This includes remaining calm around food, other animals, crowds, unusual sounds, and the many distractions encountered in daily community life.

The foundation phase also establishes the working relationship between dog and handler, teaching communication signals, attention focus, and the basic cooperation essential for successful advanced training.

Task Development and Generalization

Once foundation skills are solid, training progresses to specific task development. Each task begins with simple approximations that are gradually shaped into the final desired behavior through systematic reinforcement and practice.

Generalization training ensures that tasks learned in controlled environments transfer reliably to real-world situations. Dogs must learn to perform their tasks regardless of location, distractions, stress levels, or environmental changes that could interfere with their responses.

Ongoing Maintenance and Adaptation

Service dog training never truly ends, requiring ongoing practice and maintenance throughout the dog's working life. Tasks must be practiced regularly to maintain reliability, and new challenges may require additional training or task modification as circumstances change.

The sophisticated training that creates psychiatric service dogs represents a remarkable synthesis of animal learning science, human psychology, and practical accommodation needs. Understanding this process helps explain why these partnerships can be so transformative while also clarifying why they demand substantial investments of time, expertise, and resources to develop successfully.

The statistical realities and complex training science behind psychiatric service dog development underscore why these partnerships require such significant commitments of time, money, and expertise. Rigorous selection criteria, intensive training protocols, and ongoing maintenance create animals capable of delivering the reliable, life-changing assistance that justifies comprehensive legal protections. Yet even the most expertly trained service dog represents only half of the partnership. The daily realities of living and working with a psychiatric service dog involve lifestyle adjustments, continuous responsibilities, and challenges that many prospective handlers may not fully anticipate but must be ready to manage.

The Patience Paradox: Why Rushing Ruins Everything

When you're drowning in PTSD symptoms, when you can't leave your house without panic attacks, when nightmares steal your sleep every single night, one or two years feels like a lifetime. I understand that desperation. I lived it.

After watching my friend transform with his service dog, I wanted that independence immediately. Not in six months. Not in a year. Now. That urgency is completely understandable when you're struggling to survive each day, but it's also the very thing that can destroy your chances of ever having a successful partnership.

Here's what I've learned both as a handler and as a board member watching countless teams succeed or fail: The dogs who wash out of service work aren't usually the ones who lack intelligence or temperament. They're often the ones who were pushed too hard, too fast, by handlers who couldn't wait.

The Hidden Damage of Impatience

A common scenario illustrates the risks of premature public access work. Consider a handler whose dog has mastered basic obedience at four months of training and begins showing aptitude for anxiety alerting. The handler, encouraged by this progress and eager for independence, starts taking the dog into increasingly challenging public environments.

When the handler brings the young dog into a crowded restaurant—an environment featuring multiple stressors including noise, food smells, tight spaces, and constant movement—the dog exhibits clear signs of being overwhelmed. Rather than recognizing these stress indicators and removing the dog from the situation, the handler persists, driven by the desire to validate their dog's readiness for service work.

The consequences of this single training error can be significant and long-lasting. Dogs exposed to overwhelming environments before they're developmentally ready often develop location-specific anxieties that require months of careful counterconditioning to address. In this case, the dog developed a fear response to restaurants that necessitated extensive remedial training, setting the team's overall progress back considerably.

This pattern—early success leading to overconfidence, premature exposure to complex environments, and subsequent behavioral setbacks—represents one of the most common reasons for training delays or failures in owner-trained service dog teams. The handler's understandable desperation for a functional service dog becomes the very factor that jeopardizes the partnership's success.

Understanding Developmental Reality

A dog's brain doesn't fully mature until it's between two and three years old. Just like human children, they go through developmental stages that can't be rushed. A puppy who seems brilliant at six months might hit adolescence and temporarily "forget" everything they've learned. This is normal. This is biology. This is not failure.

Yet I've watched handlers declare their 8-month-old puppies "fully trained service dogs" and take them into situations that overwhelm their young minds. When the inevitable happens—the dog reacts badly to a new stimulus, has an accident in public, or simply shuts down from stress—these handlers often blame the dog rather than their own impatience.

The damage isn't always immediately visible. A young dog pushed beyond their emotional capacity might continue performing tasks, but stress builds like pressure in a pipe. Eventually, something gives. Sometimes it's sudden—a dog who snaps at someone after months of being overwhelmed. Sometimes it's gradual—a dog who slowly loses enthusiasm for work until they're just going through the motions.

The Program That Taught Me Patience

K9 Partners for Patriots uses a phrase that initially frustrated me but eventually became my mantra: "Slow is fast." They insisted on foundations before flashy tasks, relationships before performance, and trust before testing.

During one training session, I watched another veteran become visibly agitated because his dog wasn't progressing as quickly as mine. He started drilling commands repeatedly, his frustration evident in his voice and body language. The trainer quietly intervened: "You're not behind. Your dog is teaching you exactly what you both need to learn right now—patience."

That veteran is now one of our most successful handler teams, but it took him accepting his dog's timeline rather than imposing his own desperate need for immediate help.

The Real Timeline Nobody Talks About

Social media is filled with videos of young service dogs performing amazing tasks. What you don't see are the teams that washed out because someone confused a clever pet trick with reliable service work. Real service dog readiness isn't about task performance—it's about emotional maturity, confidence under pressure, and the kind of deep trust that only develops over time.

Grace didn't become my fully reliable service dog until she was nearly three years old. Yes, she knew her tasks earlier. Yes, she could perform them in controlled environments. But the rock-solid reliability I depend on for my independence? That took time, patience, and more setbacks than I care to count.

When Waiting Becomes Winning

The irony is that the handlers who accept the long timeline often end up with working dogs faster than those who push. Why? Because they don't have to spend months or years undoing damage caused by impatience. They don't have to rebuild trust broken by overwhelming experiences. They don't have to convince a stressed, anxious dog that work can be enjoyable again.

If you're considering a service dog and feel that desperate urgency for immediate help—and of course you do, you're suffering—please hear this: **Your future independence depends on your present patience.** The two years it takes to develop a reliable service dog will pass whether you rush or not. The only question is whether you'll have a confident, capable partner at the end of that time or a stressed, unreliable dog who represents your dashed hopes.

The partnership I have with Grace today exists because I finally learned to move at her pace rather than forcing her to match my desperation. Every moment of patience during her development now pays dividends in her reliability when I need her most. When she refused to enter that Publix all those years ago, she was teaching me the most important lesson of our partnership: Trust the process, trust the timeline, trust the dog!

Your future independence is worth the wait. Your dog's well-being demands it. And paradoxically, accepting the slow path is the fastest route to the partnership that will transform your life.

> "Your future independence depends on your present patience. The two years will pass whether you rush or not."

CHAPTER 6

Living the Partnership: Daily Realities and Lifestyle Changes

Understanding the Full Commitment

When people see me with Grace in public, they often focus on the obvious benefits—her trained tasks, the independence she provides, the companionship of a loyal partner. They don't see the daily realities of service dog ownership, the required lifestyle changes, and the ongoing commitments that extend far beyond the initial training period. Understanding these realities is crucial for anyone considering a service dog and for professionals who support handlers in their journey.

Popular culture's romanticized image of service dog partnerships rarely captures the full complexity of these relationships. Media portrayals often focus on dramatic moments of crisis intervention or heartwarming scenes of companionship, but they seldom address the mundane daily realities that shape every aspect of a handler's life. Pursuing a service dog represents not just a treatment choice but a fundamental lifestyle change that affects everything from career decisions to social relationships.

Service dog partnership isn't just about having a highly trained animal—it's about fundamentally changing how you navigate the world. Every decision, from spontaneous errands to social visits, must now factor in the needs and presence of a working dog. While the benefits often outweigh these challenges, prospective handlers must understand the full scope of what they're undertaking.

The transformation begins the moment a service dog enters your life and continues for the duration of the working partnership. Unlike other medical interventions that can be scheduled around life activities, service dogs become integral to daily existence in ways that affect every decision and interaction.

The commitment extends far beyond the handler-dog relationship to encompass family members, employers, social networks, and communities. Everyone in a handler's life must adapt to some degree to accommodate the presence of a working animal, and these adaptations aren't always smooth or immediate.

Perhaps most importantly, the commitment is not temporary or trial-based. Once a service dog partnership is established, the handler becomes responsible for that animal's welfare and working capacity for the dog's entire career. This responsibility cannot be easily transferred or temporarily suspended, creating a level of commitment that requires careful consideration before pursuing service dog training.

A Day (and Night) in the Life: Life with Grace

My "day" with Grace can actually begin before I'm even awake...

2:30 AM - Nightmare Intervention Grace starts at the edge of the bed, whining softly when she senses I'm having a nightmare. If that doesn't work, she jumps into bed and licks my face until I wake. She stays with me, providing comfort through her presence, until I settle down. Only then does she return to her kennel. This isn't trained on command—she's learned to recognize my distress signals even during sleep.

6:00 AM - Morning Routine One of us usually wakes the other around 6 AM. First priority: taking Grace outside. Then we spend 15 minutes on task training—right now I'm teaching her to turn on lights during nightmare episodes, building on her existing skills. This consistency matters; service dog training never really ends.

7:00 AM - Exercise and Enrichment Our 45-minute morning walk serves multiple purposes: physical exercise, mental stimulation for Grace, and environmental exposure that maintains her public access skills. In Florida's heat, timing is everything.

9:00 AM - Work Integration My office is on my property, which means Grace accompanies me to work every day. She settles under my desk, monitoring my stress levels while I work. Her presence is so natural now that I barely notice it—until she alerts me to rising anxiety before I'm consciously aware of it.

Afternoon - Ongoing Training We might take a midday nap together, followed by more training. Currently, I'm working to get Grace comfortable with a new treadmill—Florida heat makes daytime outdoor exercise challenging. Each new piece of equipment requires patient introduction and positive associations.

Errands - Public Access Practice Whether it's Home Depot, the grocery store, or Sam's Club, every outing is both a necessity and a training opportunity. Grace practices her public access skills while providing me the confidence and task support that makes these errands possible. The grocery store that once triggered panic attacks has become routine.

Evening - Work and Play Balance After dinner, another 15 minutes of focused task training, followed by something special—maybe a park visit for a "sniff walk" where Grace can just be a dog, or even a swim. This balance between work and enrichment is crucial for her well-being.

9:00 PM - Bedtime Routine Grace gets her evening snack and retreats to her kennel with her stuffed octopus. This routine signals the end of her official "on duty" time, though she'll still respond if I need her during the night.

This 24/7 partnership illustrates what many don't realize: Grace isn't just present during crises. She's woven into every aspect of my daily

> *life, requiring ongoing training, providing constant support, and maintaining the independence that once felt impossible.*

The Financial Reality: More Than Just Pet Ownership

Owning a service dog is significantly more expensive than typical pet ownership, with costs that continue throughout the dog's working life. While the initial training investment is substantial, the ongoing financial commitments often surprise new handlers who may have focused primarily on acquisition costs without fully considering the lifetime financial obligations.

Equipment and Gear Costs

Service dogs require specialized equipment that goes far beyond standard pet supplies. A quality service dog harness can cost $200–400, and most handlers need multiple harnesses for different situations— everyday wear, formal occasions, or weather-specific gear. While not legally required, service dog vests help reduce public questioning and typically cost $50–150 each. Many handlers find they need several vests for rotation during washing and for different weather conditions.

Working harnesses distribute weight and pressure differently than pet harnesses, providing control and communication while allowing the dog to perform tasks comfortably. Investing in quality harnesses often proves economical over time because they withstand the daily wear of public access work better than less expensive alternatives.

Then there are situational accessories that become necessary based on geographic location, climate, and specific working requirements. Living in Florida, I've learned that Grace needs protective booties during hot weather to prevent paw burns from scorching pavement. Good dog boots cost $25–75 and need replacement each year with regular use. Winter climates require different protective gear, and some handlers need additional equipment for specific task performance.

Premium Nutrition Requirements

Service dogs need consistent, high-quality nutrition to maintain their health and energy levels throughout their working careers. This typically means premium dog food that costs significantly more than grocery store brands, often $80–120 per month for a medium-to-large dog. Many handlers also provide supplements to support joint health and cognitive function, adding another $30–50 monthly to food costs.

The nutritional requirements for working dogs exceed those of pets in both quality and consistency. Service dogs cannot afford digestive upsets, energy fluctuations, or health problems caused by inconsistent or lower-quality nutrition.

This need for consistency creates logistical challenges that go beyond simple cost considerations. Handlers must plan food purchases more carefully than typical pet owners, ensuring adequate supplies during travel, emergencies, or supply chain disruptions.

Ongoing Training and Professional Support

Even after initial placement, most service dogs benefit from periodic professional training sessions to maintain skills, address behavioral challenges, or add new tasks as handlers' needs change. These sessions can cost $75–150 per hour, and many handlers schedule monthly or quarterly check-ins throughout their dog's working life.

Some handlers also participate in ongoing group training classes or specialty workshops, which provide both training value and community support. These programs may cost $200–500 per session but offer valuable opportunities to practice skills in controlled environments with professional guidance.

Professional support needs often increase rather than decrease over time, as handlers encounter new challenges, environmental changes, or evolving needs that require training modifications.

Veterinary Care and Health Management

Service dogs require more comprehensive veterinary care than typical pets because their health directly affects their handler's independence and safety. This includes frequent check-ups, preventive care, and prompt attention to any health issues that impact work performance.

Many handlers carry pet insurance, but premiums for working dogs can be higher, and coverage may exclude work-related injuries. Emergency veterinary costs can be especially challenging, as service dogs can't simply rest and recover like pets—their handlers rely on them for daily functioning, which sometimes necessitates more aggressive or costly treatment approaches.

The Education Burden

Many handlers feel an obligation to educate the public about service dogs, but this can become exhausting when every public outing includes multiple educational conversations. While I'm often happy to answer genuine questions when time permits, there are days when I just want to buy groceries without explaining Grace's training or my disability status to curious strangers.

The educational encounters typically follow predictable patterns. There's the parent who uses me as a teaching moment for their child: "See, honey, that's a working dog. Let's ask the nice man about it!" There's the fellow dog owner who wants to share their entire pet history before asking detailed questions about service dog training. There's the skeptic who launches into an interrogation about what tasks Grace performs, clearly trying to determine if she's "legitimate."

Each interaction, taken individually, seems harmless enough. The child is learning about disabilities and working dogs. The dog lover is trying to connect over a shared appreciation for animals. Even the skeptic might be reacting to negative experiences with fake service dogs. But when you're fielding these conversations at the pharmacy, the bank, the coffee shop, and the parking lot—all before 10 a.m.—the cumulative effect is draining.

The mental load is significant. While navigating my own symptoms and Grace's needs, I'm simultaneously serving as an unpaid educator, disability advocate, and ambassador for the entire service dog community. Every response I give might shape how that person treats the next service dog team they encounter. That responsibility weighs heavily, especially on difficult days when I'm barely managing my own functioning.

What makes this particularly challenging is the conflict between advocacy and self-care. I genuinely want to promote understanding and acceptance. When someone approaches with sincere curiosity and respect, I'm often energized by the opportunity to educate. I've seen how these positive interactions can transform someone's perspective, making them an ally for future handlers they encounter.

But there's no off switch for this role. Unlike professional educators who have designated work hours, handlers are "on duty" every moment we're in public with our service dogs. The grocery store at 7 p.m., after a long day, becomes another classroom. The doctor's waiting room, where I'm anxiously anticipating medical news, becomes another venue for impromptu lectures about the difference between service dogs and emotional support animals.

I've developed strategies to manage this burden while still honoring my commitment to advocacy. I carry business cards with basic information about service dogs and links to educational resources. When I'm too tired or overwhelmed for conversation, I can hand someone a card with a polite, "Here's some information that might answer your questions."

I've also learned to read situations quickly and adjust my responses accordingly. A brief "She's working right now" suffices for casual curiosity. For more persistent questioners, I might offer one educational point: "She's trained to alert me to medical episodes before I'm aware of them." This satisfies their curiosity without opening the door to extended conversation.

The challenge is balancing the desire to promote understanding and acceptance with the need to maintain personal boundaries and conserve energy for daily functioning. Some days, I have the emotional bandwidth to engage in patient education, turning encounters into positive learning experiences. Other days, particularly when my symptoms are active, every ounce of energy needs to be preserved for essential tasks.

There's also the uncomfortable reality that not all education requests come from genuine curiosity. Some people use questions as a way to challenge or gatekeep, turning what appears to be interest into an opportunity to quiz handlers about their legitimacy. Learning to distinguish between sincere curiosity and confrontational questioning has become another necessary skill in navigating public spaces.

The irony isn't lost on me: my service dog exists to help me manage my disabilities and participate more fully in public life, yet her presence often creates additional social demands that can exacerbate the very symptoms she's trained to mitigate. The anxiety of anticipating educational encounters can sometimes rival the anxiety of navigating public spaces without her.

Still, I've found meaning in this unexpected educator role. Every person who walks away with a better understanding of service dogs and invisible disabilities represents progress toward a more inclusive society. Every child who learns to respect working dogs might grow up to be an employer who accommodates handlers appropriately or a business owner who welcomes service dog teams warmly.

The key is recognizing that this education is a choice, not an obligation. While I often choose to educate, I'm not required to sacrifice my wellbeing for public understanding. Learning to say, "I'm sorry, but I'm not able to talk right now" without guilt has been as important as any task Grace has learned. Protecting my energy for essential functioning isn't selfish—it's necessary for maintaining the very partnership that enables my independence.

Physical and Emotional Demands

The Constant Responsibility

Service dogs require care and attention even when their handlers are struggling with their own mental health symptoms. During depressive episodes, when basic self-care feels overwhelming, Grace still needs to be fed, exercised, groomed, and given attention. This responsibility can be both beneficial—providing motivation and structure—and challenging when personal resources are limited.

There's also the emotional weight of being responsible for another living being whose well-being directly affects your own independence.

Managing Two Sets of Needs

A successful service dog partnership requires balancing the dog's needs with the handler's, and these don't always align perfectly. Grace might need exercise on a day when my anxiety makes leaving the house difficult, or she might be having an off day when I particularly need her task performance to be reliable.

Learning to read Grace's signals and respond to her needs while managing my own conditions takes ongoing attention and adjustment. It's a partnership that demands flexibility and communication from both sides.

The Grief of Retirement and Loss

Service dogs typically work for 8 to 10 years before retirement, and the transition can be emotionally and practically challenging. The eventual loss of a service dog represents not just the passing of a beloved companion but also the loss of independence, security, and daily support the partnership once provided.

Logistical Complications and Lifestyle Changes

The End of Spontaneous Errands

Quick trips to the store have become much more complex now that I have Grace. In Florida's heat, I can't leave her in the car while I run inside for a few items; it's legally prohibited and potentially dangerous. This means every errand, no matter how brief, requires getting Grace ready to accompany me.

On hot days, this means putting on her protective booties, which takes several minutes and requires cooperation from a dog who's learned that booties mean hot pavement walks. Simple errands now require planning, preparation, and significantly more time than they did before Grace joined my life.

Travel and Transportation Challenges

Travel with a service dog involves additional planning and costs that can transform simple trips into complex logistical operations. Airlines accommodate service dogs in the cabin, but flights must be booked with advance notice, and navigating airports with a dog requires extra time and patience. Hotels must be selected based on their accommodation quality, and even road trips require planning around the dog's needs for breaks, exercise, and relief opportunities.

Car travel means ensuring Grace has appropriate restraints for safety, adequate ventilation and climate control, and emergency supplies in case of unexpected delays.

Social Relationship Impacts

Having a service dog can affect social relationships in unexpected ways. Some friends and family members may not want dogs in their homes due to allergies, cleanliness concerns, or personal preferences. This can limit social visits or require advance planning and negotiation that didn't exist before.

Some social activities become more complicated when they involve environments that might be challenging for service dogs—crowded concerts, beach outings, or outdoor events where the dog's comfort and safety must be considered alongside the handler's social interests.

Emergency Preparedness and Crisis Planning

One aspect of service dog partnership that few handlers adequately consider until they face it is how emergencies fundamentally complicate what are already complex logistics. Unlike other medical equipment that can be easily transported or temporarily replaced, service dogs require specialized planning that must account for both the handler's needs and the dog's welfare during crisis situations.

Natural Disasters and Evacuation Planning

Living in Florida, I've learned that hurricane season requires different preparation strategies than I needed before Grace. The "grab and go" emergency planning that works for individuals becomes significantly more complex when your independence depends on a 70-pound working dog who cannot be left behind.

Emergency shelters present particular challenges. While the ADA requires that service dogs be accommodated in emergency shelters, the reality often involves overcrowded facilities where stressed, displaced people may not understand or respect service dog working protocols. Grace's training helps her remain calm in chaotic environments, but even well-trained service dogs can become overwhelmed by the unique stressors of disaster situations—unfamiliar locations, large crowds of distressed people, irregular schedules, and limited space for normal routines.

The Federal Emergency Management Agency (FEMA) recommends that service dog handlers maintain emergency kits that include at least seven days of food and water for their dogs, current photographs, medical records, vaccination documentation, and any medications the dog requires. However, handlers also need backup plans for situations where immediate evacuation prevents gathering these supplies.

I maintain emergency kits in multiple locations—my home, my car, and with trusted family members—ensuring that Grace's needs can be met regardless of where we are when disaster strikes. Each kit includes her food (in sealed containers that won't spoil), bottled water, her medications, copies of her health records, and familiar items like her regular leash and a comfort toy that can help reduce stress in unfamiliar environments.

Medical Emergencies and Handler Incapacitation

Perhaps the most challenging emergency scenario involves the handler becoming suddenly unable to care for their service dog due to medical crisis, accident, or hospitalization. Unlike family pets, service dogs cannot simply be dropped off at boarding facilities—their specialized training, working status, and the handler's dependence on them require more thoughtful contingency planning.

Every service dog handler should have a written emergency care plan that designated individuals can access and implement. This plan should identify who will care for the dog, where the dog will stay, and how to maintain the dog's training and working status during the handler's incapacitation. The designated emergency caregiver should be familiar with the dog's routine, commands, and special needs.

I've discussed these arrangements with my wife and a close friend who both understand Grace's needs and capabilities. They know her feeding schedule, her commands, her behavioral expectations, and how to contact her veterinarian and trainer if issues arise. More importantly, they understand that Grace isn't a pet during these situations—she's medical equipment that I'll need to resume my independence as soon as possible.

Financial Crisis and Economic Emergencies

Economic emergencies create unique challenges for service dog handlers whose financial situations may suddenly change due to job loss, medical expenses, or other unforeseen circumstances. The ongoing costs of maintaining a working dog—quality food, veterinary care, insurance, equipment replacement—don't pause during financial difficulties, yet these expenses may become impossible to maintain.

Unlike other medical equipment, service dogs cannot be temporarily disconnected or put on hold during financial stress. Inadequate nutrition, delayed veterinary care, or inability to replace worn equipment can compromise the dog's working ability precisely when the handler may need that support most to navigate challenging circumstances.

Financial emergency planning should include identifying resources for veterinary care assistance, food banks that serve pets, and organizations that provide financial assistance for service dog maintenance. Some service dog organizations offer ongoing support for their graduates during financial crises, while local disability organizations may have emergency assistance programs.

Family Crisis and Support System Disruption

Service dog handlers often depend on informal support networks that can be disrupted during family crises—divorce, death of family members, or family conflicts. These disruptions can eliminate backup care arrangements, financial support, or simply the understanding environment that makes service dog partnership manageable.

Family crises can also affect the service dog's training and behavior. Dogs are sensitive to household stress and may become anxious or confused when normal routines are disrupted or when emotional dynamics change dramatically. Maintaining consistent training and care during personal upheaval requires advance planning and often professional support.

Creating Effective Emergency Plans

Effective emergency planning begins with realistic assessment of potential scenarios and honest evaluation of current resources and limitations. The plan should be written, accessible to designated emergency contacts, and updated regularly as circumstances change.

Key elements include: identification of emergency caregivers and backup caregivers, current contact information for veterinarians and trainers, copies of all medical and training records stored in multiple locations, financial resources or insurance for emergency veterinary care, and specific instructions for maintaining the dog's training during the handler's absence.

The emergency plan should also address communication needs—how emergency contacts can reach the handler's medical team, service dog organization, or other relevant professionals who may need to coordinate care or provide guidance during crisis situations.

Regular review and practice of emergency plans help identify gaps or problems before they become critical. This might involve testing communication systems, verifying that emergency contacts can handle the dog successfully, or ensuring that emergency supplies remain current and accessible.

Emergency preparedness for service dog teams requires more complex planning than typical emergency preparation, but the investment pays dividends in confidence and capability when crisis situations arise. Understanding and preparing for these scenarios is as essential as any other aspect of a successful service dog partnership.

CHAPTER 7

Public Visibility and Social Challenges

The Challenge of Public Visibility

One of the most significant adjustments for many handlers is the loss of anonymity that comes with having a service dog. Every public outing becomes a potentially educational or confrontational experience, and constant attention can be exhausting for people who prefer to blend into crowds.

> "Every public outing becomes a potentially educational or confrontational experience."

Unwanted Attention and Interactions

Grace and I can't enter a store, restaurant, or public space without drawing attention. People stare, point, whisper, and frequently approach with questions or requests to pet her. While many of these interactions are well-meaning, they can be overwhelming when you're simply trying to accomplish routine errands.

The constant attention transforms routine activities into public performances, where handlers must be prepared to educate, deflect, or manage interactions instead of focusing solely on their intended tasks.

Some days, I feel like I'm wearing a sign that announces my disability status to everyone around me. This can be particularly challenging for people with invisible disabilities who may have spent years successfully managing their conditions privately.

Dealing with Skepticism and Harassment

Not all public attention is positive or well-intentioned. I've faced skeptical questioning about whether I "really" need a service dog because my disabilities aren't visible. Some people have demanded documentation, challenged my access rights, or made disparaging comments about people who "abuse" the service dog system.

Occasionally, people deliberately try to distract Grace by making sounds, calling her name, or even attempting to pet her while walking past us. These interactions require constant vigilance and can turn routine errands into stressful experiences that leave me feeling drained and defensive.

The Visibility Dilemma: When Attention-Seeking Undermines Advocacy

During a routine Walmart trip, I encountered a service dog team that made me pause. The standard poodle—and let me be clear, poodles make excellent service dogs—was dyed in rainbow colors, wearing boots indoors, sporting goggles with no sun in sight, and covered in what seemed like twenty patches and rhinestone accessories. When shoppers inevitably stared and children approached, the handler became visibly upset about the attention her dog was receiving.

I found myself caught between empathy and frustration. As handlers, we all have the right to present ourselves and our dogs however we choose. Self-expression is important, and there's no rule saying service dogs must be invisible.

The Unintended Consequences

Here's the uncomfortable truth: When a service dog team draws excessive attention through elaborate presentations, it affects all of us. That Walmart manager who sees a rainbow-colored dog covered in bling may be less welcoming to the next handler who enters with a professionally presented working dog. The customers who witness a handler seeking attention, only to become angry when they receive it, might become skeptical of all service dog teams.

The Balance Between Rights and Responsibility

This isn't about judging personal choices or suggesting there's only one "right" way to present a service dog team. Handlers have every right to dye their dog purple, add decorative patches, or express their personality through their dog's appearance. That's not the question.

The question is whether we have a responsibility to consider how our choices affect the broader service dog community. When we make choices that invite attention and then react negatively to that attention, what message does that send about all handlers? When we prioritize self-expression over professional presentation, how does that impact public perception of service dogs as medical equipment?

Finding Middle Ground

I'm not suggesting all service dogs should look identical or that handlers should suppress their personalities. Grace wears a simple vest with minimal patches, but that's my choice based on my goal of moving through public spaces with minimal interaction. Other handlers might add a fun patch or two that expresses their personality while maintaining a professional appearance.

The key is intentionality. If you choose to draw attention through your dog's appearance, be prepared to handle that attention gracefully. If you prefer minimal interaction, consider how your presentation choices align with that goal. Most importantly, remember that every public interaction shapes the perception of the entire service dog community.

The Professional Standard

In my work with K9 Partners for Patriots, we discuss "professional presentation" not as a rigid rule but as a concept worth considering.

Just as you might dress differently for a job interview than a beach day, there's value in thinking about how we present our working dogs in public spaces.

This doesn't mean boring or invisible. It means thoughtful. It means considering whether that twentieth patch or the one that drops the "F" bomb adds value or just invites questions you don't want to answer. It means asking whether those decorative accessories enhance your dog's ability to work or create distractions for both the dog and the public.

Creating Positive Change

Rather than criticizing handlers who make different choices, I try to model the behavior I hope to see. When Grace and I navigate public spaces professionally and courteously, when we demonstrate that service dogs can be both visible and unobtrusive, when we handle questions with patience and education—we're creating positive associations that benefit everyone.

The reality is that we're all ambassadors for the service dog community, whether we chose that role or not. Every interaction shapes public perception. Every team that presents professionally and behaves appropriately makes it easier for the next handler. Every team that turns their dog into a spectacle and then complains about the attention makes it harder.

We don't have to be perfect, and we don't have to be invisible. But perhaps we owe it to each other—and to the future handlers who will come after us—to be mindful of the impact our choices have on the community we're all part of, whether we like it or not.

The Visibility Paradox: When Your Service Dog Outs Your Invisible Disability

For most of my adult life, I've navigated the world with invisible wounds. My PTSD, anxiety, and traumatic brain injury don't manifest in ways that strangers can see. I don't use a wheelchair, carry a white cane, or bear visible scars that might signal to others that I'm managing a disability. This invisibility has been both a blessing and a curse—allowing me to choose when and how to disclose my conditions, but also subjecting me to skepticism when I've needed accommodation or understanding.

Then Grace entered my life, and everything changed.

The moment I clip on her service dog vest and step into public, my carefully managed privacy evaporates. What was once invisible becomes immediately, unavoidably visible to every person we encounter. This transformation represents one of the most profound and least discussed adjustments that handlers of psychiatric service dogs must navigate.

The Loss of Chosen Disclosure

Before Grace, I had complete control over who knew about my mental health conditions. I could choose to share my story with trusted friends, disclose to employers when seeking accommodation, or keep my struggles private in casual social situations. These were deliberate choices made on my timeline, when I felt safe and ready.

Now, that choice has been replaced by constant, involuntary disclosure. The grocery store clerk, the restaurant server, the stranger in the elevator—they all know something about my medical status simply by observing Grace's presence. They may not know the specifics of PTSD or understand the complexity of my conditions, but they know I have some form of disability that requires accommodation.

This shift affects different aspects of life in unexpected ways. Professional networking events, for instance, used to be spaces where I could present myself based on my expertise and experience. Now, initial conversations often center on Grace rather than my four decades as a data analyst. While most people are well-meaning in their curiosity, the focus on my disability rather than my professional capabilities can be frustrating and limiting.

The Assumption Game

The visible presence of a service dog combined with an invisible disability creates a perfect storm for public assumptions. When people see someone with a guide dog, the dog's purpose is immediately apparent. When they see Grace with me—an old guy who is still physically capable—their minds race to fill in the blanks.

I've been subjected to a startling array of assumptions from strangers who feel entitled to guess at my medical history. Some assume all veterans with service dogs have PTSD, reducing the complex landscape of military service-connected disabilities to a single diagnosis. Others, noting my apparent physical health, jump to conclusions about "fake" service dogs or handlers gaming the system for special privileges.

Women handlers often face different but equally problematic assumptions, with strangers assuming their dogs are for anxiety disorders even when they might be trained for entirely different tasks. Younger handlers frequently hear variations of "you're too young to need a service dog," as if disability respects age boundaries.

These assumptions extend beyond mere curiosity. They affect how seriously people take our need for accommodation, whether businesses respect our access rights, and how we're treated in professional and social settings. The invisible nature of our disabilities, made partially visible by our dogs, seems to invite public speculation in ways that more apparent disabilities do not.

Navigating Professional Spaces

The professional implications of this visibility deserve particular attention. Many individuals with psychiatric disabilities have spent years developing coping strategies that allow them to function in workplace environments without disclosure. The addition of a service dog makes this impossible, forcing a level of openness about mental health that can affect career trajectories, workplace relationships, and professional opportunities.

I've spoken with handlers who report being passed over for positions that require public speaking or client interaction, with employers making assumptions about their capabilities based on the presence of their service dogs. Others have found that colleagues treat them differently after they begin bringing their service dogs to work, with professional relationships shifting to include an unwanted element of caretaking or concern.

The challenge is particularly acute in fields where mental health stigma remains strong. Military and law enforcement veterans, for instance, may face additional scrutiny when their service dogs make their psychiatric disabilities visible in professional contexts that have traditionally viewed mental health challenges as weaknesses.

The Relief and Grief of Visibility

The emotional impact of this transition from invisible to visible disability is complex and often contradictory. Many handlers, myself included, experience both relief and grief in this transformation.

The relief comes from no longer needing to hide or minimize our struggles. There's exhaustion in constantly masking symptoms, in pretending that grocery stores don't trigger hypervigilance or that crowded spaces don't provoke panic. Grace's presence provides a visible explanation for the accommodations I need, eliminating the need to justify or explain my limitations repeatedly.

Yet there's also grief for the loss of privacy, for the ability to be seen first as a professional, a parent, a community member, rather than as someone with a disability. Some handlers describe mourning their ability to "pass" as a non-disabled person; to choose when their medical status becomes part of their identity in others' eyes.

Strategies for Managing Visibility

Through my own experience and conversations with other handlers, I've identified several strategies for managing this visibility paradox. First, developing a prepared narrative helps. When people ask about Grace, I have a brief, professional response that provides information without inviting further intrusion: "She's a medical alert service dog who helps me manage a neurological condition."

Setting boundaries becomes crucial. While education is important, we're not obligated to become walking encyclopedias about service dogs or our specific disabilities. Learning to redirect conversations politely but firmly helps maintain some control over how much we disclose.

Building support networks with other handlers who understand this unique challenge provides essential validation and practical advice. Online communities and local handler groups offer spaces where the visibility paradox is understood rather than questioned.

Finding Balance

Ultimately, living with this paradox requires finding a personal balance between the benefits our service dogs provide and the privacy we sacrifice. For me, Grace's alerts, grounding presence, and task performance far outweigh the discomfort of involuntary disclosure. The independence she provides is worth the visibility, even when that visibility brings unwanted attention or assumptions.

However, this calculation is deeply personal. Prospective handlers need to understand that getting a psychiatric service dog means accepting a fundamental change in how they navigate public perception of their disability. The dog that provides crucial support for invisible symptoms simultaneously makes those symptoms visible to a world that may not understand or accept them readily.

The invisibility of psychiatric disabilities has shaped my life in profound ways—sometimes protecting me from stigma, sometimes subjecting me to disbelief, always requiring careful navigation of disclosure and privacy. Grace has changed that navigation entirely, replacing chosen disclosure with constant visibility. Understanding and preparing for this transformation is as important as any task training or public access preparation in the journey toward a successful psychiatric service dog partnership.

CHAPTER 8

The Extended Partnership - Planning and Challenges

Family Dynamics and Relationship Impacts

One of the most significant but least discussed aspects of a service dog partnership is how it affects the entire family system. When I decided to pursue a psychiatric service dog, the decision wasn't mine alone to make. Susan and I had been married for over 30 years at that point, and when we first got married, we made an explicit agreement: no pets. While I often joke that Grace isn't a pet but a working dog, the reality is that I would never have moved forward with this decision without my wife's full agreement and support.

> "Pursuing a service dog affects everyone in your household, and successful partnerships require family-wide commitment."

This represents something crucial that prospective handlers need to understand: pursuing a service dog affects everyone in your household, and successful partnerships require family-wide commitment and understanding. I'm a family-first person, and there needs to be that kind of respect and consideration when making decisions that will fundamentally change how your household operates.

The Household Dynamic Shift

When Grace came into our lives, she changed everything—our routines, our living space, our travel plans, and even our social interactions. Susan suddenly found herself living with a working animal that had different rules, different needs, and different expectations than a typical pet.

These changes require patience, understanding, and ongoing communication. Family members may feel like they're walking on eggshells at first, unsure of what they can and can't do around the service dog.

The Question of Ownership and Decision-Making

This brings up what might be a controversial but necessary point: the service dog belongs to the handler, not to the family as a whole. Grace is my dog, and I am the only one who can make decisions about her care, training, veterinary needs, and working protocols. This isn't about being possessive or controlling; it's about maintaining the integrity of a working partnership that directly affects my health and safety.

My wife loves Grace, and Grace has certainly bonded with Susan in wonderful ways. However, Susan understands that Grace's primary relationship is with me and that I need to maintain full authority over decisions that affect Grace's training, behavior, and work responsibilities.

This dynamic can be challenging for families to navigate, particularly when children are involved. Kids naturally want to play with dogs, pet them, and include them in family activities. However, service dogs require different boundaries than family pets.

Communication and Ongoing Adjustment

Perhaps the most crucial element of successful family integration is ongoing communication. Susan and I regularly talk about how the partnership affects our relationship, household routines, and daily life. We discuss challenges as they arise and work together to find solutions that support both my need for Grace's assistance and our family's overall well-being.

Susan has become an advocate for our partnership in social situations, helping to educate friends and family about appropriate interactions with Grace and supporting my access rights when we encounter challenges in public.

Making the Decision Together

For prospective handlers who are married or in committed relationships, the decision to pursue a service dog should be made together, with a clear understanding of what the commitment entails. This includes honest discussions about the financial investment, lifestyle changes, time commitment, and household dynamic shifts that will occur.

The goal isn't to create rigid hierarchies or exclude family members from the service dog's life, but to ensure that everyone understands their role in supporting a partnership that provides essential medical assistance.

Building Your Support Network: A Guide for Family and Friends

While the previous section explored how service dog partnerships affect family dynamics from the handler's perspective, family members and friends often need specific guidance on how to provide meaningful support without inadvertently undermining the working relationship or the handler's independence.

Understanding Your Role as a Support Person

The most important principle for family members and friends is understanding that the service dog belongs to and works for the handler exclusively, even when the animal becomes beloved by the entire family. This isn't about being possessive or exclusionary—it's about maintaining the integrity of a working partnership that directly affects the handler's safety and independence.

Support persons should never give commands to the service dog, attempt to redirect the dog's behavior, or interfere with the working relationship without explicit direction from the handler. Even well-meaning interventions can confuse the dog about who to respond to during critical situations or disrupt carefully established communication patterns between handler and dog.

Susan, my wife, describes her role as "supporting the partnership, not managing it." She's learned Grace's routines and needs so she can help when asked, but she never attempts to handle Grace's training, behavioral issues, or care decisions. This distinction has proven crucial for maintaining both our marriage and Grace's working effectiveness.

Practical Ways to Support the Partnership

Family members can provide valuable practical support that enhances rather than competes with the service dog partnership. This might include helping with household logistics that become more complex with a working dog, providing transportation assistance during veterinary appointments, or offering emotional support during challenging training periods.

Effective practical support requires understanding the handler's specific needs and preferences rather than making assumptions about what would be helpful. Some handlers appreciate help with dog-related household tasks like grooming or exercise, while others prefer to maintain complete control over all aspects of their dog's care.

Financial support, when appropriate and welcomed, can significantly ease the burden of service dog ownership. This might involve contributing to veterinary expenses, helping with equipment replacement costs, or supporting ongoing training needs. However, financial assistance should be offered respectfully and without strings attached that could compromise the handler's autonomy over their dog's care.

Learning Appropriate Interaction Boundaries

Family members and friends must learn different interaction rules for service dogs compared to family pets. This includes not feeding the dog without permission, avoiding play or excitement that might interfere with working focus, and respecting the dog's working status even during family gatherings or social events.

Children in the household need clear, consistent guidance about appropriate behavior around working dogs. While service dogs can often enjoy play and affection during off-duty times, children must learn to recognize when the dog is working and should not be disturbed. This education benefits both the service dog partnership and the children's understanding of disability accommodation.

Extended family members and friends who see the dog less frequently may need repeated education about appropriate interaction. Family gatherings can be particularly challenging when multiple people want to interact with the service dog without understanding the working relationship or proper boundaries.

Supporting the Handler's Independence

One of the most challenging aspects of supporting someone with a service dog is finding the balance between offering help and maintaining their hard-won independence. The goal of service dog partnership is increased autonomy, and well-meaning family members can sometimes undermine this by being overly protective or helpful.

Effective support involves asking before offering assistance, respecting the handler's decisions about their own capabilities, and understanding that the service dog may enable the handler to accomplish things they couldn't do before. Family members should celebrate these increases in independence rather than continuing to treat the handler as if they require the same level of assistance they needed before their service dog partnership.

This balance becomes particularly important during the adjustment period when handlers are learning to trust their new capabilities. Family members who continue operating under old assumptions about the handler's limitations may inadvertently discourage the independence the service dog is meant to foster.

Advocacy and Public Support

Family members can serve as valuable advocates for service dog teams, particularly in public situations where the handler might face inappropriate questioning or access challenges. This support should be offered when welcomed by the handler and should focus on education rather than confrontation.

Effective advocacy involves understanding service dog rights and responsibilities, being prepared to provide factual information about ADA protections, and supporting the handler's own advocacy efforts rather than taking over the interaction. Some handlers appreciate having family members handle public education while they focus on managing their symptoms, while others prefer to maintain control over all advocacy interactions.

Family members can also help by modeling appropriate behavior toward the service dog team in public, demonstrating respectful interactions that others can observe and emulate.

Emergency Planning and Backup Support

Family members play crucial roles in emergency planning for service dog teams. This includes understanding basic care requirements for the dog, knowing how to contact veterinarians and trainers, and being prepared to provide temporary care if the handler becomes unable to manage their dog's needs.

Emergency support planning should include clear protocols for different types of crises, contact information for all relevant professionals, and understanding of the dog's routine and special needs. Family members should be familiar with the dog's commands, feeding schedule, medication requirements, and behavioral expectations.

However, emergency planning should also respect the handler's autonomy and avoid creating dependency on family assistance for routine care. The goal is to provide backup support while maintaining the handler's primary responsibility for their service dog partnership.

Long-Term Relationship Maintenance

Supporting a service dog partnership is a long-term commitment that evolves as the handler's needs change, the dog ages, and family circumstances shift. Family members should expect their support role to change over time and remain flexible about how they can most effectively contribute to the partnership's success.

This long-term perspective includes understanding that service dog partnerships typically last 8–10 years, followed by retirement transitions that may require additional family support. Planning for these transitions and understanding the emotional complexity involved helps family members provide appropriate support throughout the partnership lifecycle.

Supporting Through Challenges

Service dog partnerships aren't always smooth, and family members may need to provide support during training difficulties, health challenges, or public access problems. This support should focus on emotional encouragement and practical assistance while avoiding attempts to solve problems that require professional intervention.

Family members can help by listening without judgment, offering perspective during difficult periods, and connecting handlers with appropriate professional resources when challenges exceed family expertise. The goal is to be a source of stability and encouragement rather than trying to fix problems that require specialized knowledge.

Communication and Ongoing Adaptation

Effective support requires ongoing communication about needs, boundaries, and changing circumstances. Family members should regularly check in about how they can be helpful while respecting the handler's autonomy and the working nature of the service dog relationship.

This communication should include discussion about how family events, travel plans, and household decisions might affect the service dog partnership, ensuring that the dog's needs and working requirements are considered in family planning without allowing them to dominate all family decisions.

The most effective family support networks understand that their role is to enhance the handler's independence and the service dog partnership's success, not to manage or control either. When family members and friends understand and embrace this supportive rather than directive role, they contribute significantly to the long-term success and sustainability of psychiatric service dog partnerships.

Planning for Retirement and Succession

One of the most emotionally and practically challenging aspects of a service dog partnership—and one that few handlers adequately prepare for—is the eventual retirement of their working dog. Unlike other medical equipment that can be replaced when it wears out, service dogs are living beings with whom handlers develop profound emotional bonds over years of daily partnership.

The Reality of Working Life Spans

Service dogs typically work for 8 to 10 years before retirement, though this timeline can vary significantly based on the dog's health, the physical demands of their work, and the handler's changing needs. For psychiatric service dogs, whose work is often less physically demanding than mobility assistance, working careers may extend slightly longer. Still, handlers should plan for retirement to begin sometime between the ages of 8 and 12.

Grace is currently almost four years old, and while she's in her prime working years, I've already begun thinking about what retirement will look like for both of us. This isn't because I anticipate problems, but because the transition requires planning that can't be done effectively when it becomes an immediate necessity.

Recognizing Subtle Signs of Declining Work Capacity

Through my work with K9 Partners for Patriots and observations of other handlers, I've learned that the transition from peak working ability to retirement readiness often involves subtle changes that handlers must learn to recognize objectively. Unlike sudden injuries or obvious illnesses, work capacity decline typically develops gradually over months or years.

Physical signs that experienced handlers report include increased reluctance to perform physically demanding tasks, longer recovery times after busy days, changes in gait or movement patterns, or decreased enthusiasm for work that previously excited the dog. Some dogs begin seeking more rest during the day or show less alertness during routine monitoring tasks.

Behavioral changes can be even more subtle. Dogs might continue performing tasks correctly, but with less precision or reliability. They may become more easily distracted in public environments where they previously maintained perfect focus or show increased anxiety in situations they once handled confidently. Some working dogs begin prioritizing their own comfort over their handler's needs—seeking shade on hot days instead of maintaining a working position, or lying down during long standing periods when they previously remained alert.

The challenge for handlers is distinguishing between temporary changes due to illness, stress, or environmental factors versus permanent changes that signal retirement readiness. A dog having difficulties due to allergies or household disruption differs significantly from a dog showing consistent decline over several months.

The Emotional Journey Through Retirement

For those of us whose dogs are still working, retirement represents one of our deepest fears—returning to previous levels of limitation and dependence after years of hard-won independence. Conversations with handlers who have navigated retirement reveal that the grief process often begins long before the actual retirement decision, creating a complex emotional landscape that many find surprisingly difficult to navigate.

Unlike the clear grief of losing a beloved pet, service dog retirement involves mourning the loss of independence, security, and daily support while simultaneously celebrating the dog's years of faithful service. Many handlers report feeling guilty about their grief during retirement, believing they should be purely happy that their dog can enjoy well-deserved rest. However, the reality involves mourning a relationship that has provided daily safety and confidence for nearly a decade.

Some handlers experience what might be called "retirement denial," continuing to work dogs past their optimal retirement timeline because accepting the need for change feels overwhelming. Others make premature retirement decisions based on temporary health issues that could be resolved with veterinary care, robbing both themselves and their dogs of additional productive working years.

When Loss Becomes Real: Learning to Embrace Vulnerability

The reality of losing a service dog became starkly apparent to me during my training at K9P4P, though not in the way I'd expected. During one of our training sessions, I learned what had happened to a friend of mine—a veteran I had known for years who had partnered with his service dog for almost ten years. This man had struggled with drug and alcohol abuse for much of his adult life, but after receiving his service dog, he'd entered recovery and maintained sobriety successfully for years. The partnership had been transformative—not just for his PTSD symptoms, but for his entire approach to life and health.

Then, without warning, his service dog became ill and died. Within months, this veteran had relapsed into substance use, and eventually, he took his own life.

When I learned what had happened to him, it triggered something profound in me. The phrase "there but for the grace of God" kept running through my mind as I looked at Grace, who was still learning her tasks but had already become essential to my daily functioning. The thought of losing her—and potentially losing the independence and confidence she was helping me build—was almost paralyzing.

I seriously considered dropping out of the program. The vulnerability felt overwhelming. How could I become so dependent on another living being whose life span was inevitably shorter than mine? What would happen to me when Grace aged out of service or, God forbid, became ill or injured?

It was Damian, K9P4P's counselor, who helped me work through this fear and continue with training. He didn't minimize the reality that service dog partnerships do end, and that those transitions can be incredibly difficult. Instead, he helped me understand that this vulnerability—this interdependence—was part of what made the partnerships so powerful. The key was acknowledging the risk while building the supports and plans that would help me navigate transitions when they inevitably came.

That conversation changed how I approached my partnership with Grace. Rather than trying to protect myself from caring too deeply or becoming too dependent, I learned to embrace the relationship while simultaneously preparing for its eventual evolution. This perspective has shaped every aspect of how I think about retirement planning, succession dogs, and the support systems that need to be in place throughout a service dog's career.

Financial Planning for Retirement

Retired service dogs often require increased veterinary care due to age-related health issues, while handlers simultaneously face the expense of obtaining and training a successor dog. This financial double burden can be overwhelming if not planned for in advance.

Many experienced handlers recommend establishing dedicated savings accounts for retirement and succession planning, setting aside money monthly throughout their working dog's career. The key is beginning this financial planning early rather than waiting until retirement becomes imminent. The investment in professional consultation during retirement transitions often determines the success or failure of the process.

The Successor Dog Timeline

Most experts recommend beginning the process of identifying and training a successor dog one to two years before the current service dog's anticipated retirement. This timeline allows for adequate training while providing overlap that can ease the transition for handlers who may be anxious about the change.

The overlap period can actually be beneficial for both dogs and handlers. The retiring dog can help train the successor by modeling appropriate behavior, while handlers can gradually transition responsibilities from the older dog to the younger one.

Managing Multi-Dog Dynamics During Transition

Handlers who have managed overlap periods emphasize the importance of careful management to prevent confusion, resource guarding, or inappropriate role modeling. The retiring dog may feel jealous of the attention the new dog receives, while the successor dog must learn to ignore the former working dog's distracting behaviors.

Clear household rules become essential during this transition. The retired dog needs to understand they are no longer responsible for working tasks, while the new dog must learn their responsibilities without interference. Some handlers find it helpful to maintain different equipment—harnesses, leashes, toys—for each dog to help both animals understand their respective roles.

The Retired Dog's Adjustment Process

Handlers who have transitioned dogs to retirement report that understanding the dog's perspective helps support the animal through what can be a confusing change. Dogs who have spent years being hyper-attentive to their handler's needs may initially struggle with being "off duty." Some retired dogs continue attempting to perform their former tasks, becoming anxious when prevented from working or confused about their changing role in the household.

One K9P4P graduate described how his retired dog initially became depressed during retirement because the animal's sense of purpose had been so tied to working responsibilities. Working with a trainer, the handler helped his dog understand a new role as a beloved family pet, gradually redirecting protective instincts into appropriate play and companionship behaviors.

Other retired dogs adjust more easily, seeming relieved to be freed from the constant responsibility of monitoring their handler's condition. These dogs may sleep more deeply, play more enthusiastically, and engage in typical pet behaviors they had suppressed during working years.

The Critical Role of Support Networks

Experienced handlers consistently emphasize that successful retirement transitions require strong support networks established well before retirement becomes necessary. These networks should include family members who understand the emotional and practical challenges involved, fellow handlers who can provide advice and encouragement from personal experience, and professional trainers or organizations that offer retirement transition support.

Many service dog organizations, such as K9P4P, maintain ongoing relationships with their graduates specifically to support retirement transitions, offering guidance on timing decisions, assistance with successor dog selection, or resources for retired dog placement if handlers cannot maintain multiple dogs.

Handler support groups—both online and local—provide invaluable peer support during retirement transitions. These communities offer practical advice from others who have navigated similar experiences, emotional support during difficult adjustment periods, and reassurance that the challenges of transition are normal and manageable.

Common Transition Mistakes and Prevention Strategies

Observations of multiple retirement transitions reveal predictable mistakes that can be avoided with advance planning and professional guidance. One common error involves immediately treating the retired service dog as a pet without transitional support, which can cause confusion and behavioral regression.

Another frequent mistake is expecting the successor dog to immediately provide the same level of support as the retiring dog, without accounting for the time needed to develop the deep partnership that makes service dog work most effective. New working relationships require months or even years to reach the intuitive communication level that seasoned partnerships develop.

Most successful transitions benefit from guidance from the original training organization, professional trainers familiar with service dog retirement, or support groups of handlers who have experienced similar transitions.

Honoring the Partnership

Retirement ceremonies or recognition activities can help handlers process the emotional transition while celebrating their dog's years of service. Many handlers find that properly honoring their retired dog's service helps them feel more positive about the transition and more ready to build a new working partnership.

Planning for retirement and succession is one of the most challenging aspects of a service dog partnership, but it's also one of the most important. Handlers who approach this transition with realistic preparation, adequate resources, and emotional support often find that the process, while difficult, ultimately strengthens their confidence in maintaining independence throughout their lives with the support of successive canine partners.

The Ongoing Commitment to Training

Maintenance and Skill Development

Service dog training doesn't end at placement; it requires ongoing maintenance and development throughout the dog's working life. Grace and I practice her tasks regularly to maintain reliability, work on new skills as my needs change, and address any behavioral challenges that emerge over time.

Adapting to Changing Needs

As mental health conditions fluctuate and life circumstances change, service dogs may need additional training or task modifications. This requires handlers to understand their dog's capabilities and limitations while advocating for appropriate training support when needed.

Technology and Modern Service Dog Management

As someone with over 40 years of experience in data science and statistical analysis, I've approached service dog partnership with the same systematic, data-driven mindset I bring to complex healthcare challenges. The intersection of technology and service dog management offers significant opportunities for improving outcomes, though handlers must carefully evaluate which tools provide genuine value versus those that simply add complexity to an already demanding partnership.

Digital Training and Task Logging

Consistent record-keeping proves essential for maintaining service dog training and identifying patterns in performance, health, or behavior changes. Traditional paper logs work, but digital solutions offer advantages in organization, analysis, and sharing with veterinarians or trainers when issues arise.

Several mobile applications have been developed specifically for service dog handlers, though adoption rates remain relatively low due to privacy concerns and the additional time required for data entry.

The most useful applications typically include task performance tracking, behavioral incident recording, training session logs, and health monitoring features.

I maintain digital records of Grace's task performance using a simple spreadsheet system that tracks the frequency and effectiveness of her alerts, any environmental factors that affect her work, and patterns in my own symptoms that correlate with her behavioral changes. This data proves invaluable during veterinary visits or training consultations, providing objective information rather than relying solely on memory.

However, the key is finding systems that genuinely improve partnership management rather than creating additional administrative burden. Many handlers start with elaborate tracking systems only to abandon them when the data entry requirements become overwhelming during periods of increased symptoms or life stress.

Health and Veterinary Record Management

Digital health record systems offer significant advantages for service dog management, particularly given the specialized veterinary care these animals require. Cloud-based systems ensure records remain accessible during emergencies, travel, or when consulting with new veterinary providers.

Effective digital health management typically includes vaccination records and schedules, medication tracking and dosing histories, weight and body condition monitoring, behavioral health assessments, and emergency contact information for veterinarians and trainers. Some handlers also track correlation between their own symptom patterns and their dog's health or behavior changes.

The challenge lies in choosing systems that provide adequate security for sensitive information while remaining accessible when needed. Many veterinary practices now offer patient portals that allow handlers to access their dog's records electronically, though these systems vary significantly in functionality and ease of use.

Safety and Monitoring Technologies

GPS tracking technology has become increasingly sophisticated and affordable, offering peace of mind for handlers who worry about their service dogs going missing or being stolen. Modern GPS collars provide real-time location tracking, activity monitoring, and emergency alerts when dogs leave designated safe areas.

However, handlers must balance safety benefits with practical considerations including battery life, collar comfort for working dogs, monthly service fees, and the reality that GPS tracking doesn't prevent theft or loss—it only helps locate animals after problems occur.

Some handlers use GPS tracking during specific high-risk activities such as travel, outdoor recreation, or when training in unfamiliar environments. Others maintain tracking systems continuously as insurance against unexpected separation. The decision often depends on individual risk tolerance, lifestyle factors, and financial considerations.

Activity monitoring features in modern GPS devices can also provide health insights by tracking changes in exercise patterns, sleep quality, or daily activity levels that might indicate developing health issues before they become clinically apparent.

Communication and Emergency Systems

Modern communication technology offers several options for service dog handlers who need emergency assistance or want to maintain contact with support networks. Medical alert systems can be programmed to include information about service dogs, ensuring emergency responders understand that the handler has a working animal that requires accommodation.

Smartphone applications designed for individuals with disabilities often include features relevant to service dog handlers, such as emergency contact systems that can alert family members or medical providers, GPS location sharing for safety purposes, and quick access to important medical information including service dog details.

Some handlers maintain digital copies of essential documents—ADA information, veterinary records, emergency contact lists—in cloud storage systems accessible from any device. This ensures critical information remains available during emergencies when physical documents might not be accessible.

Training and Educational Technology

Online training resources have revolutionized access to professional service dog education, particularly for handlers in rural areas or those pursuing owner-training approaches. Video-based training programs allow handlers to learn techniques from experienced trainers, practice skills at their own pace, and review complex concepts as needed.

However, technology cannot replace hands-on professional guidance for complex training challenges or behavioral issues. The most effective use of educational technology involves combining online resources with periodic in-person consultation to ensure proper technique and objective assessment of progress.

Virtual reality training environments are beginning to emerge as tools for exposing service dogs to challenging scenarios in controlled settings. While still experimental, these technologies might eventually provide safe ways to practice responses to emergency situations, crowded environments, or other high-stress scenarios that are difficult to replicate in traditional training.

Privacy and Security Considerations

The proliferation of digital tools for service dog management raises important privacy and security concerns that handlers must carefully consider. Service dog information reveals sensitive details about disabilities, daily routines, and personal vulnerabilities that could be misused if data security is compromised.

Handlers should carefully review privacy policies for any applications or services they use, understand how their data will be stored and shared, and consider whether the benefits of digital tools justify the potential privacy risks. Many handlers choose to limit their use of technology-based management tools specifically because of these concerns.

Cloud-based systems, while convenient, create additional privacy risks compared to local storage options. However, local storage creates risks of data loss during device failure or damage. The optimal approach often involves hybrid systems that provide both convenience and appropriate security.

Evaluating Technology Solutions

The service dog technology market includes many products of varying quality and utility. Handlers should approach new technologies with healthy skepticism, focusing on solutions that address genuine needs rather than creating new problems or dependencies.

Effective evaluation criteria include whether the technology solves a real problem experienced by the handler, whether the benefits justify the cost and complexity, whether the system integrates well with existing routines and workflows, and whether adequate customer support exists for troubleshooting and maintenance.

Many handlers benefit from starting with simple, low-cost solutions before investing in more complex systems. This approach allows evaluation of genuine utility before making significant financial commitments to technological solutions.

Future Developments and Considerations

Emerging technologies may offer additional benefits for service dog partnerships, though handlers should be cautious about adopting experimental systems that lack proven track records. Artificial intelligence applications might eventually provide more sophisticated health monitoring or training support, though these developments remain largely theoretical.

The integration of service dog information with broader healthcare technology systems could improve coordination between veterinary care, mental health treatment, and service dog training. However, such integration must carefully balance potential benefits with privacy protection and system complexity.

Technology should enhance rather than complicate service dog partnerships. The most valuable technological tools are often the simplest ones that address specific practical needs without creating additional administrative burden or privacy risks. As the field continues evolving, handlers benefit from maintaining a thoughtful, selective approach to adopting new technologies while remaining open to innovations that genuinely improve partnership outcomes.

Multi-Dog Household Challenges

One aspect of service dog ownership that often catches handlers off guard is the impact of having other dogs in the household. Many people considering service dogs already have beloved pet dogs, and the dynamics between a highly trained working dog and typical household pets can create unexpected challenges.

Behavioral Influence and Training Degradation

Dogs are remarkably social learners who constantly observe and mimic the behavior of other dogs in their environment. Grace's impeccable public access behavior and task reliability can be undermined by living with dogs that haven't received the same level of training.

The Challenge of Different Standards

The behavioral expectations for service dogs are significantly higher than for typical pets. Grace must remain calm and focused in crowded restaurants, while pet dogs might be allowed to seek attention from family members during meals.

Maintaining these different behavioral standards within the same household requires careful management and clear boundaries.

Management Strategies and Household Dynamics

Successfully managing service dogs alongside pet dogs requires deliberate strategies and household rules that protect the service dog's training while maintaining fair treatment for all animals. Many handlers find they need to increase training and enrichment for their pet dogs to prevent behavioral problems and maintain household harmony.

Professional Guidance for Multi-Dog Success

Handlers who already have pets and are considering a service dog benefit from professional consultation about household management strategies. The key is recognizing that successful multi-dog households with service dogs require more intentional management than typical pet ownership.

Finding Balance: Challenges and Rewards

Despite these challenges, the benefits of service dog partnership often far outweigh the difficulties for handlers whose needs align well with what service dogs can provide. The key is understanding that a successful partnership requires ongoing commitment, financial resources, and lifestyle adjustments that go far beyond the initial placement period.

For me, the independence Grace provides, the confidence I've gained in public spaces, and the specific task support she offers make the challenges manageable and worthwhile. However, prospective handlers need realistic expectations about what service dog ownership entails in order to make informed decisions about whether this option aligns with their needs, capabilities, and circumstances.

CHAPTER 9

Supporting Service Dog Teams: A Guide for Professionals, Businesses, and Educational Institutions

Integrating Service Dogs into Treatment Planning

As a mental health professional, you're likely to encounter clients who either have psychiatric service dogs or are considering one. Understanding how these partnerships function can enhance your ability to provide comprehensive care and help you avoid common misconceptions that might inadvertently undermine the therapeutic relationship.

> "Psychiatric service dogs are never intended to replace traditional mental health treatment—they enhance it."

Service Dogs as Treatment Adjuncts, Not Replacements

The most important principle to understand is that psychiatric service dogs are never intended to replace traditional mental health treatment. Instead, they function as sophisticated assistive technology that can enhance a person's ability to implement coping strategies, maintain independence, and participate more fully in treatment and daily life activities.

Think of a service dog as you would a mobility aid for someone with physical disabilities; it's a tool that increases functional capacity without addressing the underlying condition. A psychiatric service dog might help someone with severe agoraphobia navigate public spaces more successfully. However, the underlying anxiety disorder still requires therapeutic intervention to address root causes and develop comprehensive coping strategies.

This perspective helps frame service dogs appropriately within treatment planning. Rather than viewing the dog as competing with therapeutic interventions, you can explore how the dog's trained tasks might support your client's treatment goals or enable them to practice skills in real-world settings that might otherwise be too overwhelming.

Documentation and Assessment Considerations

Clients seeking psychiatric service dogs will often need documentation from mental health professionals as part of the application process. Understanding what constitutes appropriate documentation allows you to provide proper support while maintaining professional boundaries.

Adequate documentation should establish that the client has a qualifying disability under the ADA, describe the functional limitations caused by that disability, and explain how specific service dog tasks might address those limitations. However, avoid making a judgment about whether the person should get a service dog—that typically falls outside the scope of practice and is not required by most application processes.

> **CLINICIANS:** Document limitations and how tasks address them. Avoid judging whether someone "should" get a service dog.

For example, instead of writing "John would benefit from a psychiatric service dog," more appropriate documentation might state: "John's PTSD symptoms include severe hypervigilance and panic responses in crowded environments, which significantly limit his ability to access community resources and maintain employment. These symptoms might be addressed through environmental assessment and crowd navigation tasks that psychiatric service dogs can be trained to perform."

Understanding the Handler's Experience

Clients with psychiatric service dogs face unique challenges that differ from those of other service dog handlers. Unlike guide dogs or mobility assistance dogs, psychiatric service dogs often perform tasks that aren't immediately visible to observers, which can lead to access challenges and social skepticism.

Your clients may encounter frequent questioning about their dog's legitimacy, inappropriate touching or feeding of their working animal, or even outright denial of access to public accommodations. These experiences can be especially difficult for individuals with mental health conditions who may already struggle with social anxiety or feel stigmatized by their disabilities.

Understanding these challenges enables you to provide appropriate support and validation while exploring how such experiences might affect your client's mental health and treatment progress. Some clients may need help developing assertiveness skills to advocate for their access rights, while others might benefit from processing the emotional impact of public skepticism about their disabilities.

Clinical Considerations and Red Flags

Appropriate Candidates for Psychiatric Service Dogs

Not everyone with a mental health condition is an appropriate candidate for a psychiatric service dog, and part of your role may involve helping clients realistically assess whether this option aligns with their needs, capabilities, and circumstances.

Appropriate candidates typically have stable housing, the financial resources to support a working dog throughout its lifetime, and the physical and emotional capacity to care for an animal while managing their own condition. They should have specific, identifiable functional limitations that could be addressed through trained tasks and should be engaged in ongoing mental health treatment.

Red flags may include unrealistic expectations about what service dogs can do, active substance use that could interfere with consistent care, unstable housing or finances, or motivations focused primarily on gaining public accommodation rather than addressing functional limitations.

The Adjustment Period Reality

Even successful service dog placements involve significant adjustment periods that can temporarily increase stress and require additional support. New handlers must learn to integrate the dog's care into their daily routines, navigate public access situations, and adapt to being more visible in their communities.

Some clients encounter unexpected challenges during this transition. The increased social attention that comes with having a service dog can be overwhelming for individuals with social anxiety. The responsibility of caring for a working animal can feel burdensome during depressive episodes. Advocating for access rights can be emotionally exhausting for people who already feel marginalized.

Preparing clients for these realities and providing ongoing support during the adjustment period can significantly improve outcomes and help prevent partnership failures—not because of poor dog training, but due to inadequate preparation for the lifestyle changes involved.

Working with Service Dog Organizations

Collaboration Opportunities

Many service dog organizations welcome collaboration with mental health professionals, recognizing that successful partnerships often require ongoing therapeutic support. Some programs include mental health consultations as part of their application or training processes, while others offer continuing education opportunities for providers who work with their graduates.

Building relationships with reputable service dog organizations in your area can benefit your clients by giving you referral resources and helping you better understand the realities of various training approaches. These connections can also help you stay informed about legal developments, training innovations, and funding opportunities that may support your clients.

Supporting Clients Through the Application Process

The application process for service dog programs can be lengthy and emotionally challenging. Clients may face waiting lists of several years, extensive documentation requirements, and evaluation processes that can feel invasive or judgmental.

Your support during this time might include helping clients maintain realistic expectations, processing disappointment if applications are denied, and continuing to work on underlying conditions while waiting for placement. Some clients benefit from using the waiting period to develop specific skills—such as basic dog handling or assertiveness training—that can enhance their eventual success as handlers.

Legal and Ethical Considerations

Scope of Practice Boundaries

While you can provide appropriate documentation and support for clients pursuing service dogs, avoid making specific recommendations about training programs, individual dogs, or whether someone should pursue a service dog. These decisions involve factors outside most professionals' expertise and can create liability issues if the partnership does not succeed.

Instead, focus on helping clients understand their own needs, develop realistic expectations, and access appropriate resources to make informed decisions. You might provide information about different training approaches, help clients identify questions to ask potential programs, or support them in evaluating their readiness for the responsibilities involved.

Confidentiality Considerations

Service dog partnerships can complicate confidentiality in several ways. The visible presence of a service dog makes a client's disability status somewhat public, which may affect their comfort with community-based activities or workplace accommodations.

Some clients may need support in deciding how much information to share with employers, family members, or social contacts about their service dog and underlying conditions. Others may struggle with the loss of privacy that comes with having a disability-related accommodation that cannot be concealed.

Documentation Security

Any documentation you provide for service dog applications should be treated with the same confidentiality protections as other clinical records. However, clients should understand that this documentation may be shared with training organizations, possibly retained in their files, and could be requested in certain legal situations involving access disputes.

For Business Owners and Managers

Understanding your obligations and opportunities as a business owner or manager when it comes to accommodating psychiatric service dogs isn't just about legal compliance—it's about creating genuinely inclusive environments that welcome all community members while maintaining the professional standards your customers expect.

Creating Welcoming Policies

The most effective approach to service dog accommodation begins with staff education and clear policies that go beyond minimum legal requirements. While the ADA provides the legal framework, truly inclusive businesses create environments where service dog handlers feel genuinely welcome.

Start by training all customer-facing staff on what they can and cannot ask. Under federal law, when it's not apparent that a dog is a service animal, staff can ask only two questions: "Is this dog a service animal required because of a disability?" and "What work or task has this dog been trained to perform?" They cannot ask about the specific disability, require documentation, ask for a demonstration of tasks, or charge fees because of the service dog's presence.

> **FOR BUSINESSES:** Ask respectfully. The tone matters as much as following the legal requirements.

However, go beyond these basic legal requirements to help staff understand why this accommodation matters and how to provide it gracefully. The way these questions are asked makes an enormous difference in the handler's experience. A staff member who approaches with a genuine interest in providing good service creates an entirely different interaction than one who asks the questions in a suspicious or challenging tone.

Practical Accommodation Strategies

Simple environmental modifications can make your business significantly more accessible to service dog teams without adding costs or complications. Consider the physical layout of your space—are aisles wide enough for service dogs to navigate comfortably? Are there areas where service dog teams can settle without blocking walkways or causing congestion?

In restaurants, many handlers appreciate being seated in locations that offer space for their dogs without relegating them to isolated or less desirable areas. A corner booth or a table with extra space underneath often works well, allowing the dog to lie down comfortably while staying unobtrusive to other diners.

Retail environments benefit from clear, consistently communicated service dog policies. When customers express concern about dogs in stores, well-trained staff can explain service dog access rights while reassuring them about the animals' training and behavior standards.

Handling Challenging Situations

Not every interaction involving service dogs will be straightforward, and preparing your staff for complex situations helps protect both your business and your customers. Common challenges include other customers objecting to a dog's presence, service dogs displaying disruptive behavior, or conflicts between handlers and customers with allergies or phobias related to animals.

When customers complain about service dogs, staff should be ready to explain access rights calmly and clearly. A simple explanation like, "That's actually a service dog, trained to perform specific tasks for someone with a disability. Service dogs are allowed in all areas where customers are normally permitted," often resolves concerns without confrontation.

Service dog handlers are responsible for their dogs' behavior, and businesses have the right to ask that disruptive, aggressive, or uncontrolled animals be removed. The key is to address the behavior, not make assumptions about the dog's status. If a dog is barking excessively, acting aggressively, or not responding to its handler, you can ask for the animal to be removed while still offering to serve the customer without the dog if possible.

For Educational Institutions

K-12 Considerations

Schools face unique challenges when accommodating students with service dogs due to the extended time periods involved, the presence of other children who may be distracted or fearful, and the need to balance one student's accommodation with the educational environment for all.

Successful school accommodations typically require advance planning involving the student's family, school administration, teachers, and sometimes the service dog training organization. This planning should cover practical matters such as where the dog will relieve itself, how to handle the dog during fire drills or other emergencies, and what to do if the dog becomes ill or injured during school hours.

Student education is often key to successful integration. Age-appropriate presentations about service dogs—what they do, why they shouldn't be petted or fed, and how to behave around working animals—can help prevent many potential issues while fostering understanding and acceptance among the student body.

Higher Education Settings

Colleges and universities must accommodate students with service dogs in dormitories, classrooms, dining facilities, and all other areas where students typically have access. These accommodations require coordination across departments and careful attention to the specific needs of student handlers.

Residence hall accommodations might include single rooms, rooms with easy outdoor access for the dog's toileting needs, or adjustments to standard pet policies that affect roommate assignments. Academic accommodations could involve seating arrangements that provide space for the service dog, protocols for managing the dog during laboratory classes or clinical rotations, or emergency procedures that account for the dog's presence.

The key is to involve the student in planning accommodations while recognizing that they are the experts on their own needs and their dog's capabilities. Students should not be expected to educate the entire academic community about service dogs, though they may choose to do so to help create a more comfortable environment for themselves.

For Healthcare Facilities

Balancing Access with Medical Needs

Healthcare facilities face particularly complex accommodation challenges due to infection control requirements, patient safety concerns, and the presence of individuals with compromised immune systems or severe animal allergies.

The general principle is that service dogs should be accommodated whenever possible, with alternative arrangements made only when the dog's presence would fundamentally alter the nature of the service or create direct threats that cannot be mitigated through reasonable modifications.

Most outpatient settings can accommodate service dogs without issue. Waiting rooms, consultation offices, and treatment rooms typically pose no complications. However, certain areas—such as sterile surgical environments, isolation units, or burn treatment areas—may legitimately require alternative arrangements.

When service dogs cannot be accommodated in specific medical settings, facilities should provide alternative solutions that still ensure equal access to care. This might include shorter appointment times that allow handlers to leave their dogs in appropriate waiting areas, scheduling during less busy periods, or offering private consultation areas where handlers can maintain visual contact with their dogs.

Staff Education and Patient Interaction

Healthcare staff need clear guidance on service dog policies and procedures, both for interacting with service dog teams and for addressing questions or concerns from other patients.

Medical staff should understand that service dogs are not pets and should not be petted, fed, or otherwise engaged with unless explicitly invited by the handler. They should also recognize that a handler's disability may not be visible, and questioning the legitimacy of a service dog based on appearance is inappropriate and potentially discriminatory.

When other patients express concerns—often related to allergies or phobias—staff should be prepared to address these respectfully while maintaining proper accommodations for the service dog handler. Solutions may include adjusting seating arrangements, scheduling appointments at different times, or offering private waiting areas when available.

Community Education and Awareness

Building Understanding Through Education

Community-wide education about service dogs benefits everyone by reducing conflicts, increasing acceptance, and creating more inclusive environments for individuals with disabilities. However, effective education goes beyond basic legal requirements to build genuine understanding and acceptance.

Educational presentations for community groups, business associations, or civic organizations can address common misconceptions while offering practical guidance for everyday interactions with service dog teams. These presentations are most effective when they include personal stories from handlers, concrete examples of service dog tasks, and clear guidance about appropriate and inappropriate interactions.

Addressing Common Misconceptions

Many access challenges service dog handlers face stem from persistent misconceptions about service dogs, disability, and accommodation rights. Community education should address these misconceptions directly while providing factual information that people can remember and apply in real situations.

Common misconceptions include beliefs that service dogs must wear special vests or carry identification, that all service dogs guide blind individuals, that emotional support animals have the same access rights as service dogs, or that businesses can charge fees for service dog accommodation.

Effective community education addresses these misconceptions while emphasizing the importance of service dogs in enabling independence and community participation for individuals with disabilities.

Navigating Cultural and Religious Considerations

Service dog partnerships exist within diverse cultural and religious contexts that may influence how handlers, their families, and their communities approach these accommodations. Understanding and respecting these differences helps create more inclusive environments where all individuals can access the support they need while honoring their cultural values and religious beliefs.

Cultural Perspectives on Dogs and Disability

Different cultural backgrounds may shape attitudes toward both dogs and disability in ways that affect service dog partnerships. Some cultural traditions emphasize different relationships between humans and animals, viewing dogs primarily as working animals rather than companions, or maintaining cultural practices around cleanliness and animal contact that require thoughtful navigation.

These perspectives are not barriers to overcome but rather important considerations that require respectful accommodation and understanding. Successful service dog partnerships can develop within any cultural context when families and communities work together to find approaches that honor both cultural values and individual accommodation needs.

For example, some handlers have worked with religious leaders and cultural community members to develop protocols that allow service dogs to provide essential support while respecting cultural practices around animal contact or religious spaces. These solutions often involve creative approaches such as modified equipment, alternative positioning strategies, or community education that builds understanding about the medical necessity of service animal accommodation.

Religious Accommodation and Inclusion

Various religious traditions maintain different teachings about animals, cleanliness practices, or approaches to disability that may initially seem incompatible with service dog partnerships. However, many religious communities have found ways to provide meaningful accommodation while respecting theological principles and community practices.

Religious leaders across many faith traditions have worked with service dog handlers to develop accommodation approaches that honor both religious observance and disability rights. These solutions often emphasize the religious values of compassion, inclusion, and caring for community members with different needs.

Some religious communities have found that education about the medical necessity of service dogs helps congregation members understand these partnerships within the context of religious values about healing, support, and community care. Others have developed specific protocols for service dogs in religious spaces that respect both accommodation needs and religious practices.

Family Dynamics and Cultural Values

Cultural attitudes toward disability disclosure, family decision-making processes, and community involvement can significantly influence service dog partnerships. Some cultural traditions emphasize collective family decision-making, while others prioritize individual autonomy. Understanding these dynamics helps families navigate service dog decisions in ways that honor their cultural values.

In some cultures, public visibility of disability accommodations may conflict with traditional approaches to privacy and family honor. Service dogs, by their very nature, make invisible disabilities visible to the broader community. Families may need support in balancing individual accommodation needs with cultural values around privacy and community perception.

Successful navigation often involves engaging extended family members, community leaders, or cultural advisors in educational conversations about service dogs and their role as medical equipment rather than pets. These discussions can help build understanding and support within cultural communities while respecting traditional values.

Building Cultural Competence in Service Provision

Mental health professionals, service dog organizations, and community businesses can better serve diverse populations by developing cultural competence around these considerations. This involves understanding how cultural and religious backgrounds might influence attitudes toward service dogs while avoiding assumptions or stereotypes about any particular group.

Effective cultural competence includes asking respectful questions about cultural or religious considerations that might affect service dog partnerships, providing information in culturally appropriate ways, and working collaboratively with handlers and their families to develop accommodation approaches that honor both disability rights and cultural values.

Some service dog organizations have developed partnerships with cultural community centers, religious organizations, or community leaders to provide education and build understanding about service dog partnerships within specific cultural contexts. These partnerships often prove more effective than generic outreach because they demonstrate respect for cultural values while providing relevant information.

Successful communication often involves identifying cultural liaisons or community leaders who can help bridge language and cultural gaps while ensuring that essential information about rights, responsibilities, and resources reaches handlers and their families effectively.

Creating Inclusive Communities

The goal of cultural and religious consideration is not to create separate systems or special categories, but rather to ensure that existing service dog support systems are accessible and welcoming to individuals from all backgrounds. This involves ongoing education, respectful dialogue, and collaborative problem-solving when cultural or religious considerations create apparent conflicts with standard accommodation approaches.

Communities that successfully include service dog handlers from diverse backgrounds often develop reputations for inclusiveness that benefit everyone. These communities demonstrate that respect for cultural and religious diversity can coexist with strong disability rights protections and effective service dog accommodations.

Practical Strategies for Inclusive Practice

Organizations and communities can implement several practical strategies to improve cultural inclusiveness in service dog support. These include providing materials in multiple languages, partnering with cultural and religious organizations for community education, training staff on cultural competence, and developing flexible accommodation approaches that can honor diverse values while meeting legal requirements.

Inclusive practice also involves recognizing that cultural and religious considerations are not obstacles to overcome but rather important aspects of providing person-centered support that honors the whole individual, not just their disability or service dog needs.

Successful service dog partnerships can flourish within any cultural or religious context when communities approach these considerations with respect, creativity, and commitment to finding solutions that honor both individual accommodation needs and community values. Building this understanding benefits not only handlers from diverse backgrounds but also strengthens the entire community's capacity for inclusion and support.

Understanding Your Role in Service Dog Success

When I walk into a restaurant with Grace, my psychiatric service dog, I'm not just a customer with a pet. I'm someone whose independence, safety, and ability to participate in community life depend on a carefully trained partnership that well-meaning but inappropriate interactions can disrupt. Every person who encounters a service dog team has the opportunity to either support that partnership or undermine it, often without realizing the impact of their choices.

Public behavior toward service dog teams significantly affects our ability to function in community settings. Understanding how to interact appropriately with working teams helps create an environment where individuals with disabilities can participate fully in public life. When people don't, it can create barriers that are just as limiting as physical obstacles or discriminatory policies.

The Daily Reality of Public Interactions

Let me share what a typical public outing looks like from my perspective. When Grace and I enter a store, I'm often approached by people who want to pet her, ask about her training, or share stories about their own pets. While these interactions usually come from a place of genuine interest and kindness, they can significantly interfere with Grace's ability to do her job.

Grace is trained to monitor my anxiety levels continuously, watching for subtle changes in my breathing, posture, or behavior that indicate I'm becoming overwhelmed. When someone approaches her or calls her name, her attention shifts from me to the stranger. During that distraction, she might miss the early warning signs of an anxiety attack that could escalate into a complete panic episode.

I've had people become offended when I explain that Grace is working and shouldn't be petted. Some have argued that "all dogs like attention" or questioned whether she's really a service dog because she "looks too friendly." Others have insisted on photographing us or following us through stores to get a better look at her gear. Each of these interactions, however well-intentioned, creates stress and can interfere with Grace's trained responses.

The Difference Between Helping and Hindering

The distinction between helpful and harmful public behavior often comes down to understanding that service dogs are medical equipment, not pets. When someone touches Grace without permission, it's similar to grabbing a person's wheelchair or taking someone's medication without asking. The act may seem harmless, but it interferes with essential disability-related support.

Appropriate Public Behavior

The most helpful thing community members can do is treat service dog teams with the same respect they would show anyone. This means addressing me directly rather than talking to or about Grace, maintaining normal social distance rather than crowding us to see the dog, and resisting the urge to touch or feed her without explicit permission.

When people want to interact, the appropriate approach is to ask me directly: "Would it be okay to say hello to your dog?" or "Is there anything I can do to help?" Most of the time, I appreciate the thoughtfulness behind the question, even if the answer is no. During low-stress situations, I might be happy to let someone meet Grace briefly, but during high-anxiety periods or when she's actively performing tasks, any distraction could be problematic.

Recognizing Working Behavior

Understanding when a service dog is actively working helps community members recognize when interactions are especially inappropriate. Grace might be performing room searches when we enter new environments, positioning herself strategically in crowded spaces, or monitoring my behavior for signs of escalating anxiety. During these times, she is fully focused on her job, and any interruption could compromise my safety.

However, the challenge for observers is that psychiatric service dog tasks are often invisible. Unlike guide dogs that navigate obstacles or medical alert dogs that respond to emergencies, Grace's work often involves subtle positioning, monitoring, and preventive interventions that aren't immediately apparent to others.

Legal Protections and Consequences

Beyond the practical impact on service dog teams, inappropriate interference can have legal consequences that many people don't realize. In Florida, where I live, statute 413.08 specifically addresses interference with service animals and their handlers. The law recognizes that such interference isn't just rude behavior; it's a form of disability discrimination that can put people at risk.

Florida's Legal Framework

Under Florida law, intentionally interfering with a service dog is a misdemeanor offense that can result in fines, community service, and potential jail time. More seriously, injuring a service dog can constitute a felony, reflecting the significant investment in training and the essential medical support these animals provide—support that can't be easily replaced.

The law also protects handlers from harassment based on their disability status. This means that repeatedly questioning someone's need for a service dog, demanding documentation, or creating a hostile environment through comments or behavior can carry legal consequences beyond simply being socially inappropriate.

Nationwide Protections

Similar laws exist in most states, though specific penalties and enforcement mechanisms vary. The broader principle remains consistent: service dog teams have legal protections that extend beyond general animal welfare laws, recognizing the essential role these partnerships play in disability accommodation.

However, the goal of these laws isn't to criminalize innocent mistakes or genuine curiosity about service dogs. Rather, they provide recourse for handlers who face persistent harassment, intentional interference, or discrimination based on their disability status.

Teaching Appropriate Interactions

Educating Children

Children often have the most natural and innocent reactions to service dogs, but they also need clear guidance about appropriate behavior. When children ask about Grace, I try to use it as a teaching opportunity rather than simply saying no.

I might explain that Grace is working to help me stay safe, much like a doctor or firefighter has an important job to do. Children usually understand the idea of not interrupting someone who's working, and framing service dog interactions this way helps them understand why the dog can't be petted or played with.

Parents can support these moments by preparing children in advance. Teaching kids to ask before approaching any dog—not just service dogs—encourages good habits and helps prevent problematic encounters for working teams.

Community Education

Broader community education about service dogs benefits everyone by reducing conflicts and fostering more inclusive environments. However, effective education goes beyond simply listing rules; it involves helping people understand why these guidelines matter.

When I speak to community groups, I try to explain the difference between pet dogs and working service animals. Most people love their pets and understand that those animals can be distracted by attention from strangers. The concept becomes clearer when they realize that, for service dogs, distraction isn't just inconvenient; it can be dangerous.

The Ripple Effects of Public Behavior

Creating Welcoming Communities

When community members consistently demonstrate appropriate behavior around service dog teams, it fosters an environment where people with disabilities feel welcome and supported. This isn't just about individual interactions; it's about building communities where everyone can participate fully.

I've noticed significant differences between communities in how knowledgeable and respectful people are toward service dogs. In areas with strong public education or where service dogs are more common, interactions tend to be smoother and more appropriate. In places where service dogs are rare or where misconceptions persist, I often encounter more challenges and inappropriate questions.

Supporting Business Inclusion

Community members also play a role in supporting businesses that appropriately accommodate service dogs. When customers understand and respect service dog access rights, it becomes easier for businesses to serve everyone without conflicts or complications.

I've seen situations where other customers complained about Grace's presence in restaurants or stores, putting staff under challenging positions. But I've also experienced wonderful moments when fellow customers spoke up to educate others about service dog rights or simply showed, through their own behavior, that service dogs are welcome members of the community.

Moving Beyond Compliance to Inclusion

The Goal: Natural Acceptance

The ultimate goal isn't just legal compliance or avoiding inappropriate behavior; it's creating communities where service dog teams are accepted as a natural part of the landscape. This means moving beyond seeing service dogs as unusual or noteworthy to recognizing them as one of many accommodations that help people with disabilities participate in community life.

When this acceptance becomes natural, it benefits everyone. Handlers like me can focus on daily activities without constantly navigating inappropriate interactions or educating strangers. Community members can feel confident in their interactions without worrying about saying or doing the wrong thing. Businesses can offer seamless service without complications or conflicts.

Individual Actions, Community Impact

Every person who learns how to interact appropriately with service dog teams contributes to the broader goal of inclusion. When someone respects a working dog's space, directs questions to the handler rather than about the dog, or treats service dog teams with the same courtesy they'd extend to anyone else, they help build communities where people with disabilities can thrive.

The responsibility doesn't rest solely on handlers to educate everyone they meet, though many of us are happy to answer genuine questions when time and circumstances allow. All community members should take the initiative to educate themselves, practice respectful behavior, and support inclusive policies and practices in their businesses and organizations.

As someone whose independence has been transformed by my partnership with Grace, I can tell you these individual acts of consideration and respect make a tremendous difference. They shape whether I feel welcome in my community or like an outsider whose needs are merely tolerated. They determine whether I can run errands on my own or whether public outings become sources of stress and conflict.

Building inclusive communities isn't just about grand gestures or policy changes; it's about the daily interactions that either support or hinder people's ability to participate fully in community life. Every person who takes the time to understand and practice appropriate behavior around service dog teams plays a part in making that vision of true inclusion a reality.

CHAPTER 10

Defending Trust: The Fight Against
Fake Service Dogs

The Growing Problem of Fraudulent Service Dogs

One of the most significant challenges facing the legitimate service dog community today is the growing number of individuals who misrepresent their pets as service dogs to gain access to accommodations they're not entitled to. This isn't a minor inconvenience—it's a serious issue that creates barriers for people with genuine disabilities and undermines the public trust that legitimate service dog partnerships rely on.

Understanding the Scope of the Problem

The fake service dog phenomenon has grown dramatically over the past decade, fueled by easily obtained "service dog" vests and certificates sold online, widespread misinformation about service dog rights, and insufficient enforcement of existing regulations.[3] While exact numbers are difficult to determine, service dog training organizations, disability advocates, and business owners report encountering fraudulent service dogs with increasing frequency.[1]

The problem manifests in several ways. Some individuals purchase "service dog" gear online and present their untrained pets as legitimate service dogs to gain access to housing, transportation, or public accommodation. Others genuinely believe their emotional support animals have the same access rights as trained service dogs. Still others deliberately misrepresent their pets' status to avoid pet fees or restrictions.

The Challenge of Inadequate Training vs. Intentional Fraud

Perhaps the most complex and challenging category involves handlers with legitimate disabilities whose dogs lack adequate training to perform reliable service work. These individuals aren't committing fraud—they have genuine qualifying disabilities and sincerely believe their dogs are providing essential assistance. However, their animals may have received inadequate training, been taught by inexperienced trainers, or learned inappropriate behaviors that compromise their effectiveness as working dogs.

This category often includes well-meaning handlers who attempted owner-training without sufficient professional guidance, purchased dogs from illegitimate "service dog training" operations that promise quick results, or inherited dogs from programs that maintain lower training standards. Unlike intentional fraud, these handlers genuinely need accommodation and are often unaware that their dogs don't meet the behavioral and training standards that legitimate service work requires.

The challenge is that poorly behaved animals presented as service dogs create the same public access problems as intentionally fraudulent claims. When these dogs bark excessively, fail to respond to handler commands, or exhibit inappropriate behaviors in public spaces, they reinforce negative stereotypes about all service dogs. The crucial difference is that education, proper training resources, and support—rather than enforcement—represent the appropriate response for these situations.

Distinguishing between deliberate fraud and inadequate training matters enormously for developing effective solutions. Fraudulent handlers need consequences and enforcement. Misinformed ESA handlers need education about legal differences. But handlers with legitimate disabilities and inadequately trained dogs need access to proper training resources, professional guidance, and community support to develop successful partnerships.

Real-World Impact on Legitimate Handlers

As someone who relies on my psychiatric service dog for daily functioning, I've experienced firsthand how both fake service dogs and inadequately trained animals negatively affect the legitimate community.. When poorly behaved animals posing as service dogs cause disturbances in businesses, managers often become more suspicious and less welcoming toward all service dog teams. When untrained dogs presented as "service dogs" bite other customers, bark excessively, or eliminate inappropriately in public spaces, they reinforce harmful stereotypes about service dogs and their handlers.

The impact goes beyond inconvenience. Negative experiences with fake service dogs can lead business owners to challenge legitimate handlers more frequently, ask inappropriate questions, or create barriers to access. Some have even adopted informal policies that effectively discriminate against all service dogs due to past issues with fraudulent animals.

As a result, legitimate handlers often face increased scrutiny, skeptical questioning, and demands for "proof" that their dogs are real service animals. This is especially challenging for those with psychiatric service dogs, whose disabilities may not be visible and whose dogs' tasks may not be immediately apparent to others.

The Behavioral Consequences

Perhaps most damaging is the behavioral impact of fake service dogs on public perception. Legitimate service dogs undergo extensive training to behave appropriately in all public settings—they don't bark at other dogs, jump on people, beg for food, or eliminate indoors. When untrained pets masquerading as service dogs display these behaviors, it creates confusion about what appropriate service dog behavior actually looks like.

> "When untrained pets masquerading as service dogs misbehave, it creates confusion about what appropriate behavior looks like."

This confusion has real consequences for legitimate handlers. I've seen business staff tolerate clearly inappropriate behavior from fake service dogs while questioning legitimate handlers whose well-trained dogs are behaving exactly as they should. This inconsistency leads to unclear standards and arbitrary enforcement.

Business owners who encounter animals that clearly aren't acting like trained service dogs but are being presented as such often don't know how to respond. They may hesitate to exercise their legal right to remove disruptive animals, or they may become overly suspicious of all service dogs.

Breed-Specific Challenges

One of the most frustrating and legally complex challenges I've encountered in the service dog community is breed discrimination. While the ADA explicitly states that service dogs cannot be excluded based on breed, the reality is that handlers with certain breeds face added barriers that can complicate every aspect of their partnership.

The Legal Contradiction

The contradiction between federal service dog law and local breed-specific legislation creates a minefield for handlers. While the ADA protects service dogs of all breeds, many municipalities have breed-specific legislation (BSL) that bans or restricts certain breeds, typically those perceived as "dangerous," such as pit bulls, Rottweilers, German Shepherds, and Doberman Pinschers.

In theory, federal law supersedes local ordinances, meaning a legitimate service dog should be exempt from breed bans. In practice, handlers often find themselves fighting battles they shouldn't have to fight—educating officials who should already know the law and dealing with the stress of potential confrontations that handlers with Golden Retrievers or Labradors rarely face.

I've known handlers whose perfectly trained, gentle service dogs happen to be pit bull mixes or Rottweilers. Despite their dogs' impeccable behavior and vital service role, they face constant scrutiny, fear-based reactions, and access challenges that have nothing to do with their individual dogs' temperament or training.

> The behavioral expectations for service dogs are significantly higher than for typical pets.

Housing Hurdles

The housing search becomes exponentially more difficult when your service dog is a restricted breed. While the Fair Housing Act protects service dogs from breed restrictions, many handlers report spending months searching for housing because landlords find creative ways to deny their applications without explicitly citing breed as the reason.

One handler I know, whose psychiatric service dog happened to be a Staffordshire Terrier mix, spent six months searching for housing. Despite having excellent credit, stable income, and strong references, she received rejection after rejection. Landlords would suddenly claim the unit was "no longer available" after learning about her dog's breed, or they would impose impossible application requirements that didn't apply to other tenants.

Even when handlers do secure housing, they often face ongoing harassment from property managers or neighbors who remain convinced that certain breeds are inherently dangerous. The constant need to defend their dog's right to exist in their own home adds yet another layer of stress for people already managing mental health conditions.

Insurance Complications

Insurance presents another significant challenge. Many insurance companies maintain lists of "prohibited breeds" they won't cover or impose significantly higher premiums for these breeds. While service dogs should be exempt from these restrictions, handlers often find themselves in lengthy battles with insurers who refuse to recognize the distinction between pets and service animals.

Some handlers have reported having their homeowner's or renter's insurance canceled after the company discovered their service dog's breed, despite the dog's service status and perfect behavioral record. Others face liability insurance requirements that can add hundreds of dollars annually to their expenses, simply because their highly trained service dog happens to be a breed listed as prohibited.

Public Perception and Safety Concerns

Perhaps the most exhausting aspect of having a service dog from a "scary" breed is the constant public fear and negativity. While all service dog handlers deal with unwanted attention, those with certain breeds face an added layer of suspicion and hostility.

I've seen handlers with bully-breed service dogs followed by security in stores, asking them to leave despite explaining their rights, and even being threatened by other customers who were afraid of their dogs. One handler told me about a woman who grabbed her children and ran screaming from a restaurant when she entered with her psychiatric service dog—a well-behaved American Bulldog calmly heeling beside her.

These reactions don't just cause momentary discomfort; they can trigger the very conditions the service dog is trained to mitigate. For handlers with PTSD or anxiety disorders, facing constant confrontation and hostility can make public access feel impossible, defeating the entire purpose of having a service dog.

The Training Excellence Requirement

Handlers with breeds that face discrimination often feel pressured to maintain impossibly high standards of training and behavior. While all service dogs should be well-trained, handlers with "scary" breeds know that any minor mistake—a momentary distraction, a single bark—might be used as justification to ban all dogs of that breed.

This pressure can, in some ways, benefit the service dog community by resulting in exceptionally well-trained dogs. However, it places an unfair burden on handlers who are already managing disabilities. They must serve as perfect ambassadors not just for service dogs in general, but for their entire breed.

Choosing Your Battles

Many handlers with restricted breeds develop strategies to minimize confrontation while maintaining their rights. Some carry additional documentation about federal law supremacy, even though they're not required to. Others choose to outfit their dogs with gear that clearly emphasizes their service role, despite the fact that vests and identification are not legally mandated.

Deciding which battles to fight becomes a daily calculation. Do you take the time to educate a fearful store manager, knowing it might escalate your own anxiety? Do you file a complaint about housing discrimination, aware that it could label you as a "difficult" tenant? Do you attend the community event, anticipating that your dog's breed will draw negative attention?

Moving Forward with Confidence

Despite these challenges, many handlers successfully partner with service dogs of restricted breeds. The key is understanding your rights, preparing for potential obstacles, and building support networks with others who understand these unique difficulties.

If you're considering a service dog and the best candidate happens to be a restricted breed, don't automatically rule them out. However, enter the partnership with full awareness of the additional challenges you may face. Consider whether you have the emotional resources to cope with breed discrimination on top of managing your disability and the everyday demands of a service dog partnership.

For those already partnered with service dogs of restricted breeds, remember that your dog's excellent behavior and your professional handling help break down stereotypes and pave the way for future handlers. Every positive interaction helps change minds and challenge assumptions, even when progress feels frustratingly slow.

The Case for National Standardization

Current Legal Framework Limitations

The current legal framework under the ADA deliberately avoids requiring certification or registration for service dogs, based on the principle that such requirements could create barriers to access for people with disabilities. However, this approach was developed at a time when service dog fraud was less prevalent and the consequences of that fraud were less severe.

The ADA's current approach relies on the honor system—handlers self-attest that their dogs are service animals and describe the trained tasks. While this system protects privacy and avoids bureaucratic barriers, it also offers no mechanism for distinguishing between legitimate service dogs and fraudulent claims.

Some states have attempted to address this issue by imposing criminal penalties for service dog fraud. Still, enforcement remains difficult because businesses and law enforcement often lack the knowledge to identify fraudulent claims or the authority to require proof of legitimacy.

Benefits of National Certification

A national certification system could provide multiple benefits for the legitimate service dog community while maintaining appropriate protections for handlers' privacy and rights.

Certification could establish clear, consistent service dog training and behavior standards, creating objective criteria that businesses and the public could understand and rely on. Instead of relying on subjective impressions about whether a dog "seems" like a service dog based on appearance or breed, certification would offer verifiable evidence of legitimate status.

Such a system could also offer legal protection for handlers by creating a presumption of legitimacy, reducing inappropriate questioning and access challenges. Handlers carrying valid certification would have clear evidence of their rights, potentially minimizing conflicts and improving their access experiences.

From a business perspective, certification could provide more explicit guidance about accommodation obligations while giving managers confidence in their decisions about allowing or excluding animals from their premises.

Addressing Implementation Concerns

However, any certification system must be designed carefully to avoid creating the very barriers it aims to eliminate. The primary concern is that certification requirements could prevent people with disabilities from accessing service dogs due to cost, geographic limitations, or bureaucratic complexity.

Cost Considerations and Accessibility

The most critical implementation consideration is ensuring that certification doesn't create financial barriers for people who need service dogs. Since professional service dog training already costs $15,000–$30,000 [16,17], adding certification fees could put these partnerships out of reach for many individuals with disabilities.

Any national certification system should include provisions for covering certification costs for individuals who cannot afford them. This might involve federal funding, similar to how Medicare covers durable medical equipment, or state-based assistance programs that treat service dog certification as an essential disability accommodation.

The certification process should also accommodate different training approaches – professional programs, owner-training with professional guidance, and various hybrid models – rather than privileging any single approach to service dog development.

Maintaining Privacy Protections

Certification systems must strike a balance between verification needs and privacy protection. Handlers should not be required to disclose specific medical information or disability details beyond what's necessary to establish eligibility. The focus should remain on the dog's training and task performance, not on detailed medical documentation.

Digital certification systems could provide a solution by verifying certification validity without revealing personal medical information, much like handicapped parking permits. This would allow businesses to confirm a service dog's legitimacy without accessing sensitive details about the handler's condition or limitations.

A workable certification system might include several key components designed to verify while minimizing barriers and protecting privacy.

Training Standards and Assessment

National certification could establish minimum training standards that all service dogs must meet, regardless of their training approach. These standards would emphasize public access skills, such as appropriate behavior in public settings, reliable response to handler commands, and non-disruptive conduct around people and other animals.

Task-specific assessments could verify that dogs are capable of performing the specific work they're trained for, without requiring detailed disclosure of the handler's medical conditions. For psychiatric service dogs, this might include demonstrating the ability to interrupt specific behaviors, provide grounding assistance, or retrieve medications on command.

Renewal and Maintenance Requirements

Certification could include renewal requirements to ensure ongoing training, maintenance, and behavioral standards. This would address concerns about service dogs whose performance may decline over time due to aging, illness, or lack of continued training.

Regular recertification could be designed to minimize the burden on handlers while still verifying the dog's continued reliability. This might include annual behavioral assessments, periodic training evaluations, or veterinary certifications confirming the dog's fitness for service work.

Enforcement and Fraud Prevention

Effective certification requires strong fraud prevention measures and appropriate enforcement mechanisms. This includes secure credentialing systems that are difficult to counterfeit, clear penalties for fraudulent claims, and proper training for law enforcement and business personnel on how to enforce the rules appropriately.

At the same time, enforcement must be balanced with protections for legitimate handlers. Penalties should target intentional fraud, not minor paperwork errors or good-faith misunderstandings about certification requirements.

Alternative Approaches and Interim Solutions

While national certification remains under debate, several alternative approaches could help address the fake service dog problem without requiring comprehensive federal legislation. These solutions range from grassroots education campaigns to state-level initiatives, each with its own set of advantages and implementation challenges.

Enhanced Public Education

Comprehensive public education about legitimate service dog behavior and handler rights could help businesses and community members more effectively recognize problematic situations. This education should emphasize behavioral indicators rather than appearance-based judgments, helping people understand what appropriate service dog conduct looks like.

Business Education Initiatives

The Rocky Mountain ADA Center offers free webinars and training materials specifically designed for business owners. These topics include "Service Animals and the ADA" and "How to Handle Service Animal Access Issues."[18] These programs emphasize practical scenarios and role-playing exercises that help staff feel confident in their responses.

The Department of Justice continues to receive many questions about how the Americans with Disabilities Act (ADA) applies to service animals[19], indicating an ongoing need for education. The DOJ has responded by publishing resources, including "Frequently Asked Questions about Service Animals and the ADA "[19], to reinforce its guidance.

Many businesses could benefit from implementing internal training protocols that include service dog accommodation as part of their diversity and inclusion initiatives. Effective training materials typically include specific examples of appropriate service dog behavior versus red flags that might indicate a fake service dog.

Community Awareness Campaigns

Communities could implement education-focused approaches that might include:

- Partnerships with local media to feature service dog teams and their stories
- Educational presentations at chambers of commerce and business associations
- Development of informational materials explaining the two permissible questions
- Integration of disability awareness into broader community programs

Assistance Dogs International (ADI) facilitates the exchange of best practices, knowledge of industry trends, further education of its members and the public, and the opportunity to develop the highest standards in the assistance dog industry.[20] Organizations like ADI provide resources that communities can adapt for local education efforts.

Educational Materials and Distribution

The development of standardized educational materials has proven crucial for public education efforts. Resources available include:

- The ADA National Network has created "Service Animals and Emotional Support Animals: Where are they allowed and under what conditions?"[21] - a comprehensive guide that communities can reference
- Department of Justice guidance documents that provide authoritative information about service dog rights
- Materials from service dog organizations that explain the differences between service dogs, emotional support animals, and therapy dogs

State-Level Initiatives

Individual states have implemented various approaches to address service dog fraud while maintaining accessibility. Each state's approach reflects local priorities and political considerations.

Voluntary Registration Programs

In compliance with MCL § 37.303, the Michigan Department of Civil Rights (MDCR) provides voluntary service animal identification to qualifying applicants with disabilities and their trained service animals.[22] The Michigan program, established through Public Act 147 of 2015, offers free voluntary identification for service dog teams.

The voluntary patch and ID card are intended for visual identification only and do not grant the animal or their handler any legal privileges or protections. [22] The law explicitly states that a service dog handler cannot be denied access solely for not having an ID card. [23]

Colleges and other entities, such as local governments, may also offer voluntary registries. Many communities maintain these registries to serve public purposes, such as ensuring that emergency personnel are aware of service animals during evacuations. [19] Some registries offer benefits such as reduced dog license fees for individuals who register their service animals.

Enhanced Fraud Penalties

Michigan law[24] includes penalties for misrepresenting a pet as a service animal. California has implemented even stricter fraud penalties under California Penal Code 365.7, making it a misdemeanor to knowingly and fraudulently represent oneself as the owner or trainer of a service dog, punishable by:

- Up to six months in jail
- Fines up to $1,000
- Community service requirements

Florida Statute 413.08 includes both criminal penalties for service dog fraud and civil remedies for interference with service dog teams. On May 30, 2025, Oklahoma became the 35th state to successfully pass a law that creates penalties for misrepresenting a pet as a service animal. HB 1178, supported by Canine Companions, will take effect in November 2025. [25]

State-Level Training Support

MDCR does not have jurisdiction over complaints regarding service animals in training[22]. However, effective March 28, 2023, a new Michigan law —Public Act 75 of 2022 — requires that service animals in training be admitted into places of public accommodation in Michigan, provided they are accompanied by an animal trainer or raiser for the purpose of training or socializing the animal.[22]

Some states have developed programs to support legitimate service dog teams through various means:

- Financial assistance for training costs
- Tax credits or deductions for service dog expenses
- Support for service dog training organizations operating within the state

Industry Self-Regulation

Service dog training organizations continue to develop professional standards that could provide models for broader adoption.

Professional Standards Development

Assistance Dogs International (ADI) has become the leading authority in the Assistance Dog industry[26], establishing comprehensive standards for member organizations. ADI is accredited by Assistance Dogs International, the internationally recognized governing body that establishes industry standards and practices. [26,27] Their standards include:

- Minimum training hours (120 hours over 6 months) [11]
- Public access test requirements
- Health and temperament screening protocols
- Handler education requirements
- Ongoing support obligations

ADI fosters a collaborative global community dedicated to the highest standards of excellence for human-dog partnerships.[26] These standards apply to ADI member organizations and provide a framework that other trainers may choose to follow.

Trainer Certification Programs

The Certification Council for Professional Dog Trainers (CCPDT) offers certification programs that cover knowledge areas relevant to service dog training. Individual trainers and organizations can pursue certification or accreditation to demonstrate their commitment to professional standards.

According to the organization's website, it is a health and human welfare organization based in California. The ADUC raises funds for service dog placements and grants for industry research and development.[28] Organizations like the Assistance Dog United Campaign work to improve industry standards through funding and support.

Technology Solutions

Various technology companies have developed digital solutions for service dog verification, though adoption remains limited and voluntary.

Digital Verification Systems

Several apps and digital platforms have been created to provide voluntary verification options. These systems typically offer:

- Storage of training documentation and veterinary records
- Quick reference guides for handlers about their rights
- Educational resources for businesses and the public

However, it's important to note that these systems remain voluntary and are not universally recognized. Privacy concerns and technology access barriers affect adoption rates.

Considerations for Future Development

Any technological solution must balance several factors:

- Privacy protection for handlers' medical information
- Accessibility for handlers who may not have smartphones or internet access

- Prevention of fraudulent use of the technology itself
- Cost considerations for both handlers and verifying entities

Collaborative Approaches

Perhaps the most promising interim solutions involve multiple stakeholders collaborating to create comprehensive responses to the fake service dog problem.

Multi-Stakeholder Partnerships

Several organizations demonstrate successful collaborative approaches. NEADS is *"proud of our reputation as a pioneer, leader, and innovator"* [29] in the service dog field, working with various stakeholders, including prisons, volunteers, and community organizations to train service dogs.

Effective partnerships typically include:

- Disability advocates
- Service dog training organizations
- Business representatives
- Government officials
- Law enforcement representatives

United Educators (UE) works with its members and brokers to meet insurance coverage needs, manage risk, and efficiently resolve claims[30]. This demonstrates how industry organizations can support proper service dog accommodation through education and risk management.

Community-Based Solutions

Local communities can develop approaches tailored to their specific needs and resources. These might include:

- Business education initiatives supported by local disability organizations
- Voluntary support programs for legitimate service dog teams

- Public awareness campaigns developed with input from all stakeholders
- Coordination between local agencies to ensure consistent implementation

The variety of alternative approaches shows that addressing the fake service dog problem doesn't require waiting for federal action. Communities, states, and organizations can implement solutions that protect legitimate service dog teams while reducing fraud. The key is choosing strategies that align with local needs, resources, and political realities, all while keeping the ultimate goal in mind: ensuring that people with disabilities can access their communities with the support they need.

The complex challenge of fraudulent service dogs highlights the delicate balance between protecting access rights and maintaining public trust in the service dog system. While solutions such as enhanced education and potential certification systems offer promise, the immediate priority is to continue supporting legitimate handlers and educating communities, businesses, and institutions.

The resources and next steps outlined in the following chapter offer concrete ways for individuals, professionals, and communities to be part of the solution while promoting the continued growth and acceptance of psychiatric service dog partnerships.

CHAPTER 11

Building Connections: Resources and Support Networks

Service Dog Organizations and Programs

Veterans-Focused Organizations

K9s for Warriors[7]

The nation's largest provider of Service Dogs for Veterans with PTSD, TBI, and/or Military Sexual Trauma. They provide fully trained service dogs at no cost to qualifying veterans and offer ongoing support throughout the partnership.

Pups4Patriots (American Humane)[8]

Provides exceptionally trained service dogs at no cost to veterans and retired first responders suffering from Post-traumatic Stress Disorder and Traumatic Brain Injury. Their program includes comprehensive support services and ongoing training assistance.

K9 Partners for Patriots

Serves military veterans with service-related PTSD, traumatic brain injury, and military sexual trauma. Based in Brooksville, FL, they provide comprehensive training programs and ongoing handler support.

> "For those who navigate this path successfully, the transformation can be profound—in independence, confidence, and community connection."

NEADS World Class Service Dogs[9]
Provides service dogs to veterans with combat-related disabilities, including both physical and psychiatric conditions. They offer extensive pre-placement training and lifetime support services.

General Population Programs

Assistance Dogs International (ADI)[11]
A coalition of nonprofit programs that train and place assistance dogs. Their website provides a searchable database of accredited member programs worldwide, allowing individuals to find reputable training organizations in their geographic area.

Psychiatric Service Dog Partners[10]
A comprehensive resource for individuals pursuing psychiatric service dogs, including educational materials, training resources, and community support. They focus particularly on owner-training resources and advocacy.

Service Dog Training Schools International
Provides resources for locating legitimate service dog training programs while warning about fraudulent organizations that prey on vulnerable individuals seeking service dogs.

Legal Resources and Advocacy

Federal Resources

U.S. Department of Justice ADA Information Line
Provides authoritative information about ADA requirements, including service animal regulations. They offer publications and guidance documents, and can give clarification about specific situations.

U.S. Department of Housing and Urban Development
Provides guidance about Fair Housing Act protections for service dog handlers, including information about housing accommodations and complaint procedures.

Legal Advocacy Organizations

Disability Rights Education & Defense Fund (DREDF)

Provides legal advocacy and education on disability rights issues, including service animal access rights and accommodation disputes.

National Disability Rights Network

A network of protection and advocacy agencies that can provide legal assistance to individuals with disabilities facing service dog access challenges.

Financial Resources and Funding

Grant and Scholarship Programs

Many service dog organizations provide financial assistance through sliding scale fees, fundraising support, or outright grants. Research organizations in your area to understand their financial assistance programs.

Fundraising Resources

Platforms like GoFundMe, Kickstarter, and specialized service dog fundraising websites can help individuals raise funds for service dog training and ongoing care expenses.

Veterans Benefits

While the VA doesn't directly provide psychiatric service dogs, they do provide healthcare benefits that can include veterinary care for service dogs placed through approved programs. Contact your local VA representative for current benefit information.

Training and Educational Resources

Professional Training Resources

Certification Council for Professional Dog Trainers (CCPDT)

Provides certification for professional dog trainers and maintains directories of certified trainers who may be able to assist with service dog training.

International Association of Canine Professionals
Another source for locating professional trainers with experience in service dog work.

Owner-Training Resources

Service Dog Training Institute
Offers online courses and resources for individuals pursuing owner-training approaches to service dog development.

Psychiatric Service Dog Partners
Provides extensive educational materials, training guides, and community support specifically for psychiatric service dog handlers.

Ongoing Support and Community

Online Communities

Service Dog Forums and Social Media Groups
Multiple online communities provide peer support, training advice, and advocacy resources for service dog handlers. Look for groups that maintain professional standards and avoid commercialization.

Psychiatric Service Dog Partners Community
Offers peer support specifically for individuals with psychiatric service dogs, including resources for training challenges, access issues, and partnership maintenance.

Local Resources

Disability Resource Centers
Many communities have disability resource centers that can provide information about local service dog resources, legal assistance, and community support services.

Veterans Service Organizations
Local VFW, American Legion, and other veterans organizations often have information about service dog programs and can provide support for navigating application processes.

These comprehensive resources provide a foundation for moving forward, whether as a prospective handler, supporting professional, or community advocate. The organizations, legal references, training materials, and support networks listed here reflect the shared knowledge and dedication of a community committed to expanding access to life-changing service dog partnerships. As we conclude this guide, the focus shifts from gathering information to taking action—applying this knowledge to help build a more inclusive society where individuals with psychiatric disabilities can thrive with the support and accommodations they need and deserve.

CHAPTER 12

Final Thoughts: Moving Forward with Knowledge and Hope

This comprehensive guide represents more than just information about psychiatric service dogs—it's a roadmap toward greater independence, understanding, and community inclusion for individuals with mental health conditions. Whether you're a mental health professional seeking to better serve your clients, an individual considering whether a psychiatric service dog might help your situation, or a community member wanting to create more inclusive environments, the knowledge contained in this guide provides a foundation for informed decision-making and effective advocacy.

The journey toward a psychiatric service dog partnership isn't simple or guaranteed. The statistics are sobering, the investment is substantial, and the commitment is lifelong. However, for those who do navigate this path successfully, the transformation can be profound—not just in terms of symptom management, but in terms of reclaiming independence, rebuilding confidence, and reconnecting with community in ways that might not otherwise be possible.

> "For those who navigate this path successfully, the transformation can be profound—in independence, confidence, and community connection."

Understanding the full scope of service dog partnership helps prospective handlers make informed decisions while preparing adequately for the realities of this life-changing commitment. The challenges are real and substantial, but so are the rewards for those who approach the partnership with realistic expectations and thorough preparation.

Most importantly, remember that you're not alone in this journey. Whether you're just beginning to explore the possibility of a psychiatric service dog or you're already navigating the complexities of this partnership, there are resources, communities, and advocates ready to support you. The legal protections exist to support these partnerships, but they require knowledgeable advocacy to be effective. The training resources are available, but they require significant commitment to be successful. Community support exists, but active engagement is required to be accessible.

At the same time, we must acknowledge and address the challenges that threaten these partnerships. The growing problem of fake service dogs undermines public trust and creates barriers for legitimate handlers. Finding solutions that protect access rights while addressing fraudulent claims requires ongoing collaboration among all stakeholders—handlers, training organizations, businesses, policymakers, and the broader community.

The goal isn't just individual success; it's building a more inclusive society where all individuals with disabilities can participate fully in community life with the accommodation and support they need to thrive. Every successful psychiatric service dog partnership contributes to that larger vision, breaking down barriers and building understanding that benefits everyone.

A Window Into the Partnership

As someone whose life has been fundamentally changed by this partnership, I want to leave you with a story that captures something

I rarely get to witness—how this relationship appears to those who observe it from the outside.

Generally, I never get to see how Grace works from an outside perspective. I'm always the subject of her focus, making it difficult to step outside our relationship and observe us as others do. But last year, my wife and I were out on a pontoon boat with some friends, including Keith, who was burdened with Parkinson's disease.

We were all talking and laughing, enjoying the day on the water. Grace was lying quietly at my feet on the deck, as she typically does in social situations. During our conversation, Keith grew quiet and seemed to be experiencing some kind of distress—perhaps pain or fatigue, though he didn't say anything about it.

Without any cue from me, and without any apparent awareness on my part of Keith's situation, Grace suddenly got up from her position at my feet. She jumped onto the cushioned seating next to Keith and leaned against him, providing the same kind of comforting pressure she gives me during difficult moments.

I was stunned. I had never seen her do this before—extend her trained responses to someone else who was in distress. It was an incredible realization for me of how others see Grace and me together, and how her training has created such sophisticated awareness that she could recognize and respond to distress in another person entirely.

Keith later told me how much that moment meant to him, how Grace seemed to sense exactly what he needed when he was struggling. For me, it was a window into understanding something I'd never fully grasped: that this partnership extends beyond my individual needs to create ripples of compassion and understanding that touch everyone around us.

REMEMBER: Every successful partnership helps build understanding and acceptance for the entire community.

That moment on the boat crystallized something important about these partnerships. Though their benefits are profound, they're not just about individual accommodation or personal independence. They're about building connections, fostering understanding, and creating communities where empathy and support flow naturally between all members—human and canine alike.

This ripple effect extends in unexpected directions. When I visit elementary schools with Grace to educate children about service dogs, I'm consistently amazed by how naturally kids understand and respect boundaries. They listen intently when I explain that Grace is working and shouldn't be petted or distracted. They nod thoughtfully when I tell them how to behave around service dog teams.

What strikes me most is when these young voices pipe up with their own observations: "My mom always tries to pet dogs like yours," or "My dad says all dogs want attention." These children, some as young as six or seven, instinctively grasp concepts that many adults struggle with. They understand that working dogs have important jobs to do, that not all accommodations are visible, and that respect means giving space rather than demanding interaction.

Perhaps most hopefully, these children will go home and become teachers themselves, gently correcting adult misconceptions with the confidence and authority that only children possess. In these moments, I see the future of service dog acceptance—a generation growing up with a natural understanding of disability accommodation and respect for working partnerships.

When that first episode happened in the Publix parking lot, I was new to this partnership and confused about what was happening. I wasn't sure if Grace was just being stubborn or if there was some issue with her training. I questioned whether I was reading the situation correctly, whether I was giving her the right signals, and whether this whole endeavor was going to work.

Now, as I look back, I see that she was doing exactly what she was supposed to be doing. She recognized something in my condition that day that I couldn't yet perceive myself, and she made the decision to keep me safe by refusing to enter an environment that would have overwhelmed my already fragile state. What felt like confusion and disappointment at the time was actually my first real glimpse of the sophisticated partnership we were building.

Today, I can tell the difference between an alert and a miscue, between Grace responding to my actual needs and my own misinterpretation of her behavior. This melding of minds—this intuitive understanding that flows both ways between us—is the dividend of all those early investments: the months of training, the financial commitment, the lifestyle changes, and the patience required to learn each other's language.

That Publix parking lot was where our real partnership began—not with fanfare or dramatic intervention, but with Grace's quiet insistence that my safety mattered more than my plans. Every lesson since then has built on that foundation of trust and protection she established before I even understood what was happening.

Take the knowledge you've gained from this guide and use it as a starting point for your journey, whether that involves pursuing a service dog partnership, supporting someone else in that process, or simply becoming a more informed and inclusive community member. Whether you're taking the first steps toward exploring a psychiatric service dog partnership, working to better support someone in your life who has one, or seeking to create more inclusive spaces in your community, remember that every action matters.

THE GOAL: Building communities where all individuals can thrive with the accommodation and support they deserve.

Every conversation about mental health accommodation, every respectful interaction with a service dog team, and every effort to understand rather than judge contributes to a society where all individuals can thrive. The transformation is possible. The support is available. The community is growing stronger. The future is hopeful.

Grace may never read these words, but every page reflects something she's taught me about resilience, trust, and the profound connections possible when we commit to the work of understanding and supporting one another. That lesson extends far beyond service dog partnerships to encompass how we can all contribute to building a more compassionate, inclusive world, where what happened on that boat—spontaneous compassion, intuitive understanding, and the natural extension of care from one being to another—becomes the norm rather than the exception in how we relate to one another.

Frequently Asked Questions (FAQ)

Getting Started

Q: How do I know if I'm a good candidate for a psychiatric service dog?

A: Good candidates typically have diagnosed mental health conditions that significantly limit major life activities, stable housing and financial resources to support a working dog, engagement with mental health treatment, and specific functional limitations that could be addressed through trained tasks. The decision is highly individual and should involve consultation with both mental health professionals and service dog training organizations.

Q: What's the difference between a psychiatric service dog and an emotional support animal?

A: Psychiatric service dogs are individually trained to perform specific tasks that address their handler's disability-related limitations. Emotional support animals provide comfort through companionship but don't require task training. Only psychiatric service dogs have public access rights under the ADA.

Q: Which mental health conditions qualify for psychiatric service dogs?

A: The ADA doesn't specify particular diagnoses but requires that you have a disability that substantially limits major life activities. Common conditions include PTSD, severe anxiety disorders, major depression, bipolar disorder, autism spectrum disorders, and dissociative disorders. The key is having functional limitations that trained tasks can address, not the specific diagnosis.

Q: Do I need my doctor's permission to get a psychiatric service dog?

A: You don't need permission, but you will need documentation from a mental health professional for most training programs. This documentation should establish your qualifying disability and explain how service dog tasks might address your functional limitations.

Q: How long are the waiting lists for service dog programs?

A: Waiting lists vary widely, from six months to several years depending on the organization, your location, and your specific needs. Veteran programs often have shorter wait times due to dedicated funding. Use the waiting period to prepare financially and educationally for the partnership.

Training and Selection

Q: Can I train my own psychiatric service dog?

A: Yes, the ADA doesn't require professional training. However, owner-training is challenging and has lower success rates than professional programs. Most successful owner-trainers work with professional consultants and invest significant time and resources in the training process.

Q: What if my current pet could be trained as my service dog?

A: While possible, most pets lack the temperament and early socialization needed for service work. Professional evaluation is essential—many beloved pets simply aren't suitable for the demands of public access and task performance. Be prepared for the possibility that your pet may not be appropriate for service work.

Q: How do I choose between different training programs?

A: Research each program's accreditation status, success rates, training methods, and post-placement support. Ask about costs, timelines, and what happens if the placement doesn't work out.Visit facilities if possible and speak with recent graduates about their experiences.

Q: What happens if my service dog "washes out" of training?

A: Dogs that don't complete service training aren't failures—many become beloved family pets or working dogs in other capacities. Reputable programs should have policies about what happens to dogs that don't complete training, including options for adoption by the intended handler.

Costs and Funding

Q: How much does a psychiatric service dog cost?

A: Professionally trained service dogs typically cost $15,000-$30,000. However, many programs serving veterans provide dogs at no cost. Owner-training can be less expensive initially but still involves significant costs for training resources, veterinary care, and ongoing maintenance.

Q: Are there grants or funding sources available?

A: Some organizations offer sliding scale fees or fundraising support. Veterans may have access to programs at no cost. Individual fundraising through platforms like GoFundMe has become increasingly common.

Some insurance companies are beginning to cover service dog costs, though this remains inconsistent.

Q: What are the ongoing monthly costs of owning a service dog?

A: Expect $200-400 monthly for premium food, veterinary care, equipment replacement, and training maintenance. Emergency veterinary costs can be substantial, so many handlers carry pet insurance.

Daily Life and Practical Questions

Q: Can I leave my service dog at home sometimes?

A: Yes, you're not required to take your service dog everywhere. Many handlers leave their dogs home for brief errands, social events where the dog might be disruptive, or activities that might be stressful for the animal.

Q: What do I do if my service dog gets sick or injured?

A: You remain responsible for your service dog's veterinary care throughout its working life. Have an emergency veterinary plan and consider pet insurance. Some programs provide ongoing veterinary support for dogs they've placed.

Q: How do I handle people who want to pet or distract my service dog?

A: Politely explain that your dog is working and shouldn't be distracted. A simple "She's working right now, but thank you for asking" usually suffices. You can carry educational cards to hand out when you don't have time to talk.

Q: What if someone challenges my right to have my service dog in a business?

A: Remain calm and know your rights. Staff can ask only two questions: whether the dog is a service animal required because of a disability, and what task the dog is trained to perform. If access is still denied, ask to speak with a manager and consider filing a complaint with the Department of Justice.

Q: Can I bring my service dog to work?

A: The ADA requires employers to consider service dogs as reasonable workplace accommodations, but it's not automatically guaranteed. Success depends on your job duties, workplace environment, and whether the accommodation creates undue hardship for your employer.

Living with a Service Dog

Q: How do I explain my service dog to children?

A: Keep explanations simple and age-appropriate: "This is my working dog who helps me stay safe and healthy. She's doing an important job, so please don't pet her without asking." Most children understand the concept of not interrupting someone who's working.

Q: What if I have other pets at home?

A: Service dogs can live successfully with other pets, but it requires careful management. Your service dog must maintain higher behavioral standards, and pet dogs can sometimes interfere with service dog training. Professional guidance is often helpful for multi-dog households.

Q: How do I travel with my service dog?

A: Airlines must accommodate service dogs in the cabin without additional fees, but advance notice is required. Hotels must accept service dogs regardless of pet policies. Road trips require planning for the dog's exercise, relief, and safety needs.

Q: What about housing – can landlords still deny me?

A: Service dogs are protected under the Fair Housing Act regardless of pet policies, deposits, or breed restrictions. However, you remain liable for any damage beyond normal wear and tear, and the dog cannot pose a direct threat to others.

Advanced Questions

Q: Can I have more than one service dog?

A: The ADA allows individuals to have more than one service dog if each dog is trained to perform different tasks that address the person's disability. However, this is relatively uncommon and requires careful consideration of practical and financial implications.

Q: What happens when my service dog retires?

A: Service dogs typically work for 8-10 years before retiring. Many handlers choose to keep retired service dogs as pets while obtaining new working dogs. Plan financially and emotionally for this transition, which can be challenging but manageable with preparation.

Q: Can my service dog be trained to help with medication compliance?

A: Yes, dogs can be trained to retrieve medications, provide medication reminders at specific times, or alert family members if you don't take medications on schedule. These tasks must address functional limitations caused by your disability.

Q: What if my service dog isn't performing tasks correctly anymore?

A: Contact your trainer or program immediately. Sometimes issues are minor and easily corrected, while other times they may indicate health problems or the need for retirement. Don't wait—early intervention often prevents more serious problems.

Q: Are psychiatric service dogs allowed in hospitals and medical facilities?

A: Generally yes, though some sterile environments may require alternative arrangements. Hospitals must accommodate service dogs whenever possible and provide alternatives when the dog cannot be present during specific procedures.

Q: What should I do if my service dog is attacked by another dog?

A: Seek immediate veterinary care for your dog and medical attention for yourself if needed. Document the incident thoroughly and contact local authorities. You may have legal recourse for veterinary bills and the cost of any additional training needed.

Q: Can my family members give commands to my service dog?

A: Service dogs should respond primarily to their handler to maintain the working relationship. Family members can learn basic commands for emergencies, but routine direction should come from the handler. Discuss boundaries with your family early in the partnership.

Q: What if I move to a different state?

A: Service dog rights are federal, so legal protections remain consistent across states. However, some states have additional protections or requirements. Research your new state's laws and ensure your veterinary records and health certificates are up to date.

Q: How do I know if my mental health has improved enough that I don't need my service dog anymore?

A: This is a complex decision that should involve your mental health provider, service dog trainer, and careful self-assessment. Consider whether you can maintain your current functioning without the dog's support and what happens during potential relapses.

When Things Don't Work Out

Q: What if the service dog partnership isn't working for me?

A: Not all partnerships succeed, even with good dogs and motivated handlers. Contact your training organization for guidance. Sometimes issues can be resolved with additional training, while other times the best solution is placing the dog with another handler and exploring alternatives.

Q: Are there alternatives if I can't get a service dog?

A: Yes, consider other accommodations like emotional support animals (for housing), workplace modifications, assistive technology, or enhanced mental health treatment. Service dogs aren't the only path to independence and improved functioning.

Q: How do I cope with the loss of my service dog?

A: Losing a service dog involves both grief for a beloved companion and anxiety about managing without their support. Many handlers benefit from counseling during this transition. Plan ahead by developing other coping strategies and support systems you can rely on.

References

1. **Canine Companions for Independence, Assistance Dogs International**. Service dog handlers' experiences with poorly trained or fraudulent service dogs: international survey results. 2018. https://www.assistancedogsinternational.org/resources/service-dog-handlers-experiences/

2. **Rocky Mountain ADA Center**. Service animals and emotional support animals. https://rockymountainada.org/topics/service-animals-and-emotional-support-animals

3. **American Kennel Club**. The problem with fake service dogs. 2021. Accessed May 29, 2025. https://www.akc.org/expert-advice/news/the-problem-with-fake-service-dogs/

4. **US Department of Justice**. Americans with Disabilities Act. ADA requirements: service animals. Updated February 28, 2020. https://www.ada.gov/service_animals_2010.htm

5. **US Department of Housing and Urban Development**. Assistance animals. Accessed May 29, 2025. https://www.hud.gov/program_offices/fair_housing_equal_opp/assistance_animals

6. **Winkle M, Crowe TK, Hendrix I**. Service dogs and people with physical disabilities partnerships: a systematic review. Occup Ther Int. 2012;19(1):54-66. doi:10.1002/oti.323

7. **K9s for Warriors**. About us. https://k9sforwarriors.org/about-us/

8. **Pups4Patriots**. About us. https://www.paws4people.org/pups4patriots/

9. **NEADS World Class Service Dogs**. About us. https://www.neads.org/about/

10. **Psychiatric Service Dog Partners**. About us. https://psychdogpartners. org/about/

11. **Assistance Dogs International**. About us. https://www.assistancedogs international.org/about/

12. **US Department of Transportation**. Service animals. Updated February 28, 2022. Accessed May 29, 2025. https://www.transportation.gov/ individuals/aviation-consumer-protection/service-animals

13. **Bray EE, Levy KM, Kennedy BS, Duffy DL, Serpell JA, MacLean EL**. Predictive models of assistance dog training outcomes using the Canine Behavioral Assessment and Research Questionnaire and a standardized temperament evaluation. Front Vet Sci. 2019;6:49. doi:10.3389/ fvets.2019.00049

14. **Range F, Viranyi Z, Huber L.** Selective imitation in domestic dogs. Curr Biol. 2007;17(10):868-872. doi:10.1016/j.cub.2007.04.026

15. **Miller HC, Rayburn-Reeves R, Zentall TR**. Imitation and emulation by dogs using a bidirectional control procedure. Behav Processes. 2009;80(2):109-114. doi:10.1016/j.beproc.2008.10.004

16. **The Dog Alliance. Service dog training costs: full guide with funding tips**. October 28, 2024. Accessed May 29, 2025. https:// thedogalliance.org/cost-of-service-dog-training/

17. **Integrity, Inc.** National Service Animal Registry estimates that a service dog costs a minimum of $17,000 to nearly $40,000. June 1, 2022. https:// www.integrityinc.org/how-much-does-it-cost-to-get-a-service-dog/

18. Rocky Mountain ADA Center. Service animals and emotional support animals. Accessed January 14, 2025. https://rockymountainada.org/ topics/service-animals-and-emotional-support-animals

19. US Department of Justice. Frequently asked questions about service animals and the ADA. Updated 2020. Accessed January 14, 2025. https:// www.ada.gov/resources/service-animals-faqs/

20. Assistance Dogs International. About ADI. Accessed January 14, 2025. https://assistancedogsinternational.org/

21. ADA National Network. Service animals and emotional support animals: where are they allowed and under what conditions? Accessed January 14,

2025. https://adata.org/guide/service-animals-and-emotional-support-animals

22. Michigan Department of Civil Rights. Service animals. Accessed January 14, 2025. https://www.michigan.gov/mdcr/divisions/ada-compliance/service-animals

23. Service Dog Certifications. Michigan service dog requirements. Updated October 11, 2024. Accessed January 14, 2025. https://www.servicedogcertifications.org/michigan-service-dog-requirements/

24. Nolo. Michigan laws on service dogs and emotional support animals. Updated October 3, 2024. Accessed January 14, 2025. https://www.nolo.com/legal-encyclopedia/michigan-laws-on-service-dogs-and-emotional-support-animals.html

25. Canine Companions. Oklahoma passes service dog fraud law. May 30, 2025. Accessed January 14, 2025. https://canine.org/

26. Assistance Dogs International. ADI summary overview, vision, mission and governance. Accessed January 14, 2025. https://assistancedogsinternational.org/

27. NEADS World Class Service Dogs. About NEADS. Updated January 18, 2025. Accessed January 14, 2025. https://neads.org/about/

28. Service Dog Training School International. Grants for service dogs. Accessed January 14, 2025. https://www.servicedogtrainingschool.org/blog/grants-for-service-dogs

29. NEADS World Class Service Dogs. Service dogs since 1976. Updated January 18, 2025. Accessed January 14, 2025. https://neads.org/about/

30. United Educators. Service animals and the ADA. August 6, 2021. Accessed January 14, 2025. https://www.ue.org/risk-management/compliance/service-animals-and-the-ada/

31. **Kokocińska-Kusiak A, Woszczyło M, Zybala M, Maciocha J, Barłowska K, Dzięcioł M**. Canine olfaction: physiology, behavior, and possibilities for practical applications. *Animals (Basel)*. 2021;11(8):2463. doi:10.3390/ani11082463

32. National Institute of Mental Health. Mental illness. 2023. Accessed May 29, 2025. https://www.nimh.nih.gov/health/statistics/mental-illness

33. U.S. Department of Veterans Affairs. How common is PTSD in veterans? Updated 2018. Accessed May 29, 2025. https://www.ptsd.va.gov/understand/common/common_veterans.asp

34. O'Haire, M. E., Rodriguez, K. E., White, G., & McConnell, S. (2018). Improved Outcomes for Veterans with Posttraumatic Stress Disorder and Chronic Pain Receiving Service Dogs. *Journal of Consulting and Clinical Psychology, 86*(9), 686–694. https://doi.org/10.1037/ccp0000332

35. Leighton, S. C., Rodriguez, K. E., Jensen, C. L., MacLean, E. L., Davis, L. W., Ashbeck, E. L., Bedrick, E. J., & O'Haire, M. E. (2024). Service Dogs for Veterans and Military Members with Posttraumatic Stress Disorder: a nonrandomized controlled trial. *JAMA Network Open*, 7(6), e2414686. https://doi.org/10.1001/jamanetworkopen.2024.14686

Glossary

ADA (Americans with Disabilities Act) - Federal civil rights law that prohibits discrimination based on disability and establishes access rights for service dogs in public accommodations.

ADI (Assistance Dogs International) - Coalition of nonprofit programs that train and place assistance dogs; provides accreditation standards for member organizations.

Alert/Alerting - Trained behavior where a service dog notifies their handler of an oncoming medical episode or environmental concern before the handler is consciously aware.

Autism Assistance Dog - Service dog trained to help individuals on the autism spectrum with challenges such as sensory overload, social navigation, or safety concerns.

Blocking/Covering - Task where a service dog positions themselves as a physical barrier between their handler and other people or environmental stressors.

BSL (Breed-Specific Legislation) - Local laws that ban or restrict certain dog breeds, which may conflict with federal service dog protections.

Classical Conditioning - Learning process where dogs associate environmental cues with specific responses; used in service dog training to teach recognition of physiological changes.

Community-Based Training – Training model where handler and dog learn together from the beginning, with the handler taught to train their own dog.

Deep Pressure Therapy (DPT) – Trained task where a service dog applies body weight and pressure to help calm their handler during anxiety or panic episodes.

Direct Threat – Legal standard allowing exclusion of service dogs only when they pose significant risk of substantial harm that cannot be eliminated through reasonable modifications.

Emotional Support Animal (ESA) – Animal that provides comfort through companionship but is not trained to perform specific tasks; has limited legal protections compared to service dogs.

Fair Housing Act – Federal law protecting service dog handlers from housing discrimination, including pet policies, deposits, and breed restrictions.

Fake Service Dog – Pet fraudulently presented as a service dog, often with purchased vests or certificates, lacking legitimate training and legal status.

Guide Dog – Service dog trained to assist individuals who are blind or have severe visual impairments by navigating obstacles and providing mobility support.

Grounding – Techniques service dogs use to help handlers reconnect with their physical environment and present reality during dissociative episodes or panic attacks.

Handler – Person with a disability who is partnered with a service dog; the only person who can make decisions about the dog's care and training.

Hearing Dog – Service dog trained to alert individuals who are deaf or hard of hearing to important sounds like doorbells, alarms, or approaching vehicles.

Hypervigilance – Heightened state of alert common in PTSD where individuals constantly scan for potential threats; can be addressed through service dog environmental assessment tasks.

Interruption Task - Trained behavior where a service dog breaks destructive cycles or provides stabilizing influence during active mental health episodes.

Medical Alert Dog - Service dog trained to detect specific medical conditions such as seizures or diabetic episodes and either alert their handler or summon help.

Mobility Assistance Dog - Service dog trained to help individuals with physical disabilities by providing stability, retrieving items, or operating equipment.

Nightmare Interruption - Task where a service dog recognizes signs of sleep disturbance and gently wakes their handler using specific techniques to minimize disorientation.

Operant Conditioning - Learning process where behavior is modified through consequences; used to teach service dogs that performing specific tasks results in positive outcomes.

Owner-Training - Approach where individuals train their own service dogs, often with professional guidance, rather than receiving pre-trained animals.

Psychiatric Service Dog - Service dog trained to perform specific tasks related to mental health disabilities such as PTSD, anxiety disorders, or depression.

Public Access Rights - Legal protections allowing service dogs to accompany their handlers in public accommodations where pets are typically prohibited.

Public Access Training - Extensive training ensuring service dogs behave appropriately in all public settings, including ignoring distractions and maintaining focus on their handler.

Room Clearing/Search - Task where a service dog systematically checks new environments and reports back to their handler, addressing hypervigilance symptoms in PTSD.

SDiT (Service Dog in Training) - Dog undergoing service dog training but not yet fully trained; may have limited public access rights depending on state laws.

Section 504 - Federal law extending ADA-like protections to programs receiving federal funding, including many schools, hospitals, and social service organizations.

Seizure Response Dog - Service dog trained to assist during or after seizure episodes by providing stability, retrieving medication, or activating emergency systems.

Service Animal - Under federal law, only dogs (and in some cases miniature horses) individually trained to work or perform tasks for people with disabilities.

Task - Specific, trained behavior that a service dog performs to address their handler's disability-related limitations; multiple tasks are required for legitimate service dog status.

Therapy Dog - Animal trained to provide comfort and support to multiple people in facilities like hospitals or schools; different from service dogs and has no public access rights.

Traditional Training Model - Training approach where organizations maintain complete control over training until final handler matching and placement.

Two Questions - Only questions businesses can legally ask about service dogs: "Is this a service animal required because of a disability?" and "What task has the dog been trained to perform?"

Washout - Dog that doesn't complete service dog training due to health, behavioral, or temperament issues; often becomes pets or working dogs in other capacities.

Working Partnership - The collaborative relationship between a service dog and handler, characterized by mutual communication, trust, and shared responsibility for daily functioning.

www.ingramcontent.com/pod-product-compliance
Lightning Source LLC
Chambersburg PA
CBHW031503120626
46545CB00005B/1729